# LIVING WITH PURPOSE BIBLE STUDY

# Revelation

# LIVING WITH PURPOSE BIBLE STUDY

# Revelation

Guideposts

## A Gift from Guideposts

Thank you for your purchase! We want to express our gratitude for your support with a special gift just for you.

Dive into *Spirit Lifters*, a complimentary e-book that will fortify your faith, offering solace during challenging moments. Its 31 carefully selected scripture verses will soothe and uplift your soul.

Please use the QR code or go to **guideposts.org/ spiritlifters** to download.

**Living with Purpose Bible Study: Revelation**

Published by Guideposts
100 Reserve Road, Suite E200
Danbury, CT 06810
Guideposts.org

Cover design by Judy Ross
Interior design by Judy Ross
Cover photo by Pinopic/iStock
Typeset by Aptara, Inc.

ISBN 978-1-961442-43-6 (hardcover)
ISBN 978-1-961251-01-4 (softcover)
ISBN 978-1-961251-02-1 (epub)

Printed and bound in the United States of America
10 9 8 7 6 5 4 3 2 1

# CONTENTS

# *About Living with Purpose Bible Study*

---

For as long as humankind has existed, we have pondered our place in the universe. Poets and preachers, philosophers and scientists alike have explored the topic for generations. Our busy modern lives leave little time for contemplation, and yet we move through our lives with nagging questions in the back of our minds: *Why am I here? What am I meant to do with my life?*

Fyodor Dostoevsky wrote that the "mystery of human existence lies not in just staying alive, but in finding something to live for." You might wonder how living with purpose ties in with the Bible. That's because God's Word is a guidebook for life, and God Himself has a purpose—a unique mission—for and unique to you. Reading the Bible and seeking God through prayer are two of the main ways God speaks to people. And when we begin to seek God, when we pursue His truth, when we begin to live our lives in ways that reflect His love back to others, we begin to find that purpose. Finding our purpose is not a destination; it is a journey we'll travel until we leave this earth behind and go to our heavenly Father.

Most of us know something about the Bible. We might be able to quote verses that we memorized as kids. Many of us have read parts of it, have learned about it in Sunday school both as children and adults. But not as many of us *know* the Bible, and that is where this Bible study comes in.

"Bible study" is a term that can elicit a variety of responses. For some people, the feeling that comes is a daunting sense of intimidation, even fear, because we worry that the Bible will somehow find us wanting, less than, rejected. Maybe we've heard preachers wielding the Bible as a weapon, using it as a measuring rod and a dividing line that separates "us" from "them."

Guideposts' *Living with Purpose Bible Study* addresses these questions and concerns with a hope-filled, welcoming, inclusive voice, like the one you've grown to know and love from Guideposts' devotional books, story collections, magazines, and website.

Best of all, you'll discover that the writers of *Living with Purpose Bible Study* are experts not only in the depth of their Bible knowledge but also in sharing that knowledge in such a welcoming, winning way that you can't help but be drawn in.

The writers come alongside you as trusted friends, guiding you through each volume in that warm, inviting manner that only Guideposts could bring you.

Each volume in the study draws from five trusted translations of the Bible: the New International Version, New American Standard Bible, the Amplified Version, the English Standard Version, and the King James Version of the Bible. We encourage you to keep your favorite Bible translation on hand as you read each study chapter. The Bible passages you read act as the foundation from which the study writer's insights, information, and inspiration flow. You can read along with the writers as each chapter unfolds, or you can read all of the passages or verses included in the chapter prior to reading it. It's up to you; you can use the method that works best for you.

In addition, you'll find two distinct features to enhance your experience: "A Closer Look" entries bring context by presenting historical, geographical, or cultural information, and "Inspiration from Psalms" entries demonstrate the spiritual insights people like you have gained from their knowledge of the biblical text. We've also provided lined writing spaces at the end of each lesson for you to jot down your own thoughts, questions, discoveries, and *aha* moments that happen as you read and study.

A final note: before you read each chapter, we encourage you to pray, asking that God will open your eyes and heart to what He has to say. Our prayer for you is that you find a new or renewed sense of purpose and grow closer to God as you deepen your understanding of God's Word by enjoying this *Living with Purpose Bible Study*.

—*The Editors of Guideposts*

# An Overview of Revelation

---◆---------------◆---

The book of Revelation has a PR problem. People think of it as difficult to read, puzzling, mysterious, and even frightening. So much so that many people, even some of the staunchest, most faithful believers, avoid reading it. Revelation is a highly charged, emotional book, often controversial, because its symbolic writing is open to so many interpretations. Some preachers even refuse to preach about Revelation—preferring to leave it sitting on a dusty shelf, out of sight, or treating it as something less than the inspired Word of God, despite its accepted place in the canon since the early days of Christianity.

Revelation could also be titled "Apocalypse," a word that has entered the popular vernacular through books and movies that are inevitably about the end of the world. It's tempting to set Revelation aside and let the professionals handle it.

But never fear! We're here to tell you that, despite its arcane and byzantine reputation, the book of Revelation is a very positive, uplifting book. As the late Rev. Dr. Billy Graham pointed out, "The book of Revelation may be difficult and demanding to read, yet it is the only biblical book whose author promises a blessing to those who read it."

Written as it was, to churches who were facing terrible tests and trials from Caesar and the Roman Empire in the first century, it remains relevant for Christians today who face our own tests and trials in the twenty-first century. Revelation was meant for you, not just for Christians in the first century.

Together, we are going to ignore that reputation of being difficult and study this amazing book because it has so much to offer us.

To get a better understanding of Revelation, and to give us a firm foundation to stand on as we learn about it, we need to ask ourselves three questions a good journalist asks when writing a news story: *Who*, *When*, and *Why*. Knowing these basics will set the stage for the rest of the study.

### Who Wrote Revelation?

First-century readers were very sure of the identity of the author of Revelation. They knew him personally as John, their "brother, and companion in tribulation" (1:9, KJV). They also knew him as a prophet or "preacher." He had a special place and was highly respected among the seven churches of Asia. He was known as a unique man of God, and his word carried authority. He wrote what he saw, and since what he saw and heard came from God, his word was faithful and true (1:11, 19).

All of this simply meant that when the book of Revelation was read in the Asian churches, they felt they were hearing from a friend and that he was speaking directly to them.

The writer of this book is clearly identified as John, but as with other New Testament books, there has for centuries been a great deal of speculation as to just who this John was.

Some interpreters believe he was John, the beloved disciple, who wrote the Gospel that bears his name and the three letters of John. Other scholars suggest that this John was a Palestinian Jew who came to Asia Minor late in life.

It is obvious that John was steeped in the Old Testament because he quoted from or alluded to it 245 times. We also can tell that he was familiar with the Jewish apocalyptic books that were written between the time of Malachi and the New Testament writings. While he wrote in Greek, it is obvious that he thought in Hebrew.

The precise identity of the author is not as important as his message.

### When Was Revelation Written?

The second thing those first readers knew was *when* John wrote this book. Again, this is open to speculation. There are those who date the writing of Revelation earlier, but we shouldn't be far wrong if we set the date around AD 92–96—during the last four years of the reign of the Roman Emperor Domitian (doh-MEESH-un). The first persecution of Christians for refusal to worship the emperor took place during those years.

Church tradition—history that has been handed down from the earliest days of Christianity—has consistently taught that Emperor Domitian exiled John to a concentration camp on the Isle of Patmos. Then after the emperor's death it is believed that John was liberated and returned to Ephesus, one of the seven churches he had written to.

### Why Was Revelation Written?

The third thing those early readers knew was that the churches in the Roman province of Asia (modern-day Turkey) were going through turbulent times. Five of the seven churches had the serious internal problem of disloyalty to Christ. John was deeply concerned about the heresy—probably Gnosticism—that was assailing the churches.

The Gnostics were a group of Christians who claimed to have a special revelation from God that allowed them to also dabble in the Roman civil religion. They watered down the uniqueness of Christ, and since they considered all matter to be evil, their behavior was colored by moral compromise.

Then, too, the Christians within these churches were in severe danger because of the civil demand of emperor worship. The idea of emperor worship began in a spontaneous burst of gratitude when Caesar Augustus (27 BC–14 BC) brought peace to the ancient world. Out of gratitude the people began to deify the emperors who personified Roman peace. But for the most part, the early emperors didn't take this seriously until the time of Domitian.

When his brother Titus died in AD 81, Domitian inherited the throne, and to offset his insecurity he laid claim to being a god. Well before AD 100, six of the cities John mentioned in Revelation had imposing temples dedicated to the worship of Domitian. In fact, an ancient statue of Domitian depicted as a god has been found in Ephesus.

Domitian tolerated no opposition and required his subjects to call him "Our Lord and God." And so, as the leader of the churches in Asia Minor that opposed emperor worship, John was banished to Patmos, where, while in chains and enduring great hardship, he wrote to people who were facing prison or execution. The Roman Empire was at war with the Christian church.

## Apocalyptic Literature

The fourth thing John's readers knew was that his letter was a kind of writing known as *apocalyptic* literature. The very first word in the Greek text of Revelation is *opokalupsis* (1:1), which means to uncover, disclose, or reveal. This particular kind of writing had flourished from about 200 BC to AD 200, so John's readers would have read and understood it as well as we read our daily newspapers.

Now, if apocalypse means "revelation," what, then, is an apocalypse? The answer to that question will help us better understand some of the Old Testament prophets as well as this book of Revelation. In the Old Testament it was the grand, optimistic vision of the prophets that God was about to bring His plan for human history to a climax. It was the message that God would directly intervene in human affairs to create a new and perfect age. And so apocalypse is the unveiling through symbolic images and visions of how God will have His will done on earth as it is in heaven.

## Characteristics of Apocalyptic Literature

Since John's first readers would have so clearly understood this kind of literature, we should ask ourselves what they could have told us that would help us understand this particular book.

These first readers could have told us to watch for the literary devices that carried the apocalyptic message, such as visions, prayers, hymns, the symbolic use of numbers, word pictures, and allegory. They would tell us to take note of ecstatic feelings and experiences, a sense of urgency, and an emphasis on the end times that characterize John's letter.

Then we see that those first-century readers could have cautioned us to be aware of the basic theological ideas that are found in apocalyptic literature, such as the truth that God is in control of history, that He is not indifferent to the world, that His power is equal to the needs of our time, and that only God can initiate the end of history. We would see that the goal of history is the spiritual kingdom of God.

Finally, we would have learned from those first readers to hang on to the enduring, overarching apocalyptic message— that, while history can be divided into a number of ages, God is in control of every age. And Christians can be optimistic about God's plans. As Billy Graham said, "I have read the last page of the Bible. It is all going to turn out all right."

Ethical and spiritual principles are eternal, and there is life after death. The letter's first-century readers would have told us, too, that apocalyptic symbols are to be taken seriously but can often be interpreted in more than one way.

The important thing for us now is to move ahead in our study of this remarkable book with an open mind and a prayerful heart. There is a powerful message here for us as we attempt to live faithful Christian lives in the twenty-first-century world.

We will soon see that this book belongs to our time. It is uniquely Christian and distinctive because it is the Good News of Jesus Christ in an unusual apocalyptic form.

# The Victorious Christ and His Seven Churches

◆————————————————◆

*Dear Father, as I study this lesson on the "victorious Christ,"*
*help me to know victory in my own life. AMEN.*

## John's Introduction (1:1–8)

These first three chapters that we will cover in this lesson are
the most familiar part of Revelation and are not too hard to
understand. The first chapter contains the preface, a greeting
and a doxology (an expression of praise to God), and a vision
of Christ among the seven churches of the province of Asia.
Then chapters 2 and 3 contain letters to those seven churches.

### *The Preface*

The book opens with these words: "The revelation of Jesus
Christ, which God gave him to show to his servants the things
that must soon take place. He made it known by sending his
angel to his servant John, who bore witness to the word of God
and to the testimony of Jesus Christ, even to all that he saw.
Blessed is the one who reads aloud the words of this prophecy,
and blessed are those who hear, and who keep what is written
in it, for the time is near" (1:1–3, ESV). These opening words
of the preface tell us that this book comes from God as a
message that was formerly hidden, veiled, or secret.

The revelation, or apocalypse, is a disclosure *of* Jesus, *from* Jesus, and *about* Jesus. He is central to everything that is written. It was, of course, from heaven because there is just no other way we as humans could conceive of it.

Next, it comes through clearly that there are five links in this chain of communication. One, God is the original Author. Two, the message comes to us through Christ. Three, an angel received the word. Four, John is given the message to write down. Five, John then sends the message to the seven churches. A sixth link was added when those first-century Christians and believers of all time, including us, read the message.

John next speaks of the message—"the things that must soon take place" (1:1, ESV). In apocalyptic language, the word *soon* implies that, once God has set events in motion to bring about "the End," it could happen at any time. We humans are unable to comprehend God's sense of time, and so Christians live in constant expectation of that day when Christ will return.

Continuing in that first verse, John writes that Christ "signified" (1:1, KJV) the message. This is an important statement because it tells us right at the beginning that he is going to use *signs* as the medium to get his message through.

A sign always points to something real, but the sign and what it points to are not one and the same thing. For example, if you drive on the interstate and see a sign saying the name of a gas station and an exit number, you know that the sign is not actually the gas station. But for the sign to have any meaning you need to know that gas stations exist and trust that the sign is pointing you to the actual gas station.

In a sense, all language is symbolic, for lan~~g~~ never stands in a one-to-one relationship with rea~~l~~ what the angel "signified" to John had lots of reality to up. In fact, in verse 2 John says that what was revealed to ~~h~~ was the Word of God—the Word as given through the Old Testament prophets and by Jesus and the apostles.

Then John closes his preface by pronouncing a blessing on those who read or hear what he is writing and then act on it—"and take to heart what is written in [this prophecy]" (1:3, NIV). The wording here reflects the worship service in the early church where the reader stood and read the Scripture aloud. John is telling his readers it is important that they read and hear what he is saying, but that isn't all. For example, in the Sermon on the Mount, Jesus didn't say at the conclusion, "Congratulations if you think this is a good sermon." Rather, the idea He was getting across was, "Congratulations if you put into practice what I've said in the sermon."

We learn in this opening section something very important as we move into our study. Yes, what John is writing here has historical implications, but it is much more than that—it is God's Word to us *now*. This is why our study in this somewhat puzzling book can mean a great deal to us.

## Greetings and Doxology (1:4–8)

### The Writer and to Whom This Is Written

In the letter-writing custom of the first century, John identifies himself immediately as the writer and then indicates to whom he is writing: "John, to the seven churches in the rovince of Asia" (1:4, NIV). In all probability, John sent only one handwritten copy of this letter, but it was his intention that it be passed along and circulated among all seven of the churches. Then, after these had read it, John probably intended for them to make copies for distribution among all the other churches throughout the Roman Empire.

## A Blessing

John next moves on to another typical part of an ancient letter as he writes, "Grace and peace to you" (1:4, NIV)—grace, the undeserved blessing from God, and peace, a word of particular significance to the Jews of that time, and to the Christians because of their sense of unity and harmony with the Father. And these words are followed immediately with the source of the blessing: "from him who is and who was and who is to come, and from the seven spirits who are before his throne, and from Jesus Christ" (1:4–5, ESV).

In other words, this blessing addressed to the Christians in the seven Asian churches was from the eternal God who *is*, who *was*, and who *is to come*—He is the "I AM WHO I AM"— the God who revealed Himself to Moses in the desert (Exodus 3:1–15). He is the God of the past, the present, and the future.

The blessing is also from the Holy Spirit—the "seven Spirits." The reference here is not to a literal number but to the biblical meaning of the word *seven*—completeness, fullness. It is the fullness of the Holy Spirit that is to be with all churches in all time.

Finally, the blessing is from Jesus Christ, who was a "faithful witness" (1:5, ESV) during His earthly life, was a "faithful witness" in the lives of the Christians in the seven churches, and will be a "faithful witness" in the future in the new heaven and the new earth.

Jesus is also identified as "the firstborn of the dead, and the ruler of kings on earth" (1:5, ESV). The word of encouragement in this identification is that since Jesus was raised from the dead, Christians of all time will experience new life in the final resurrection. Also, the risen Christ is sovereign over the entire world. This is a key theme throughout the book of Revelation— Christ rules the world (11:15, 17:14, and 19:16). The idea here is that the rule of kings is temporary and weak, but the rule of the risen Christ *will be forever*—a direct challenge in the first century to the notion that Emperor Domitian was a divine ruler.

### A Burst of Praise

It is not surprising after what he has just written that John next writes words of praise: "to him be glory and power for ever and ever! Amen" (1:6, NIV). "For ever and ever" includes the past, the present, and most certainly the future: "Behold, he cometh with clouds; and every eye shall see him" (1:7, KJV). Here in verse 7, John, who was completely saturated in the Old Testament Scriptures, lifted words from Daniel 7:13 and Zechariah 12:10. It is interesting to note that in the book of Revelation, John has no less than thirty-one allusions to the book of Daniel 7.

A keystone of Christianity is the Second Coming of Christ, which John is describing so vividly here. In fact, a Christianity without the return of Christ would not be Christianity. And in verse 8 this truth is guaranteed as God identifies Himself with four names that reveal His character and describe His actions. He says, "I am the Alpha and the Omega . . . who is, and who was, and who is to come, the Almighty" (1:8, NIV). It is only in the book of Revelation that God is referred to as Alpha and Omega—the beginning and the end, or as we might put it, "the A to Z." He is the absolute Creator and Director of everything.

We have devoted considerable space to these first eight verses in our study because of their importance to all that follows in the rest of the book. John wanted to make certain that his readers clearly understood him.

## The Victorious Christ among His Seven Churches (1:9–20)

### John in Exile

After identifying himself again, John tells his readers that he has been banished to the island of Patmos because of his faithfulness to the Good News (1:9). They would have known Patmos well. The whole island was a sort of Roman concentration camp. It was twenty-five bleak square miles of volcanic hills and stone ridges located just a few miles off the coast of the province of Asia, modern Turkey. Eusebius, an early church historian, wrote that Domitian sent John there in AD 95 and that he was released eighteen months later by Emperor Nerva, Domitian's successor.

### John's Commission

John next tells us that he "was in the Spirit [in special communication with the Holy Spirit and empowered to receive and record the revelation from Jesus Christ] on the Lord's Day" (1:10, AMP), and God instructed him to note carefully what he was to see and hear so he could write it down and send it to the seven churches (1:10–11). We learn here that John "was in the Spirit." He was transported into the world of prophetic visions. We also learn that this occurred on the "Lord's day"— the only time this term is used in the New Testament— doubtless referring to Sunday, "the first day of the week."

### *The Vision of the Son of Man*

John now describes the vision that he saw (1:12–16). Most certainly, John and the Christians in the seven churches needed encouragement, the sort of encouragement that could come only through the vision of the risen Christ that John saw.

John was a prisoner in chains, existing under the poorest of conditions, and most likely working all day in the Patmos rock quarries. At the same time, the Christians in the seven churches were enduring extreme hardship and even death because of their loyalty to Christ. And as if that wasn't enough, they were having to stand against the false teaching that was assailing the churches at that time. They were involved in an intense struggle, and, along with John, this vision of Christ's power could indeed quicken their hope and give them confidence for the future.

In his vision John writes that he "saw seven golden lampstands" (1:12, NIV). These lampstands or candlesticks represented each of "the seven churches in the province of Asia" (1:4, NIV) that "Alpha and Omega" instructed John to send this book to. But it also represents the complete and universal church wherever it is found.

It may be a coincidence, who knows? But if you were to take a map and draw a line through the location of the seven ancient churches of Asia, it would resemble in rough form a seven-branched lampstand. But the important thing to John's first readers is that they would immediately associate it with the lampstand that had been a part of the Jewish temple in Jerusalem. But here John wants them and us to see the lampstands as symbolic of the new spiritual temple, the church.

Even as the lampstand in the tabernacle and later in the temple—God's center of worship for His people—was a source of light, so we as Christians are to be light bearers in our places of worship and in the world. The imagery here is reminiscent of Jesus's words, "I am the light of the world. Whoever follows me will not walk in darkness, but will have the light of life" (John 8:12, ESV). It is clear here that the source of our light is Jesus Christ.

And so it is not surprising that in John's vision he saw "in the midst of the seven candlesticks [lampstands] *one like unto the Son of man*" (1:13, KJV, italics added). This is indeed a portrait of Christ based on the colorful words in Daniel 7:13, "I saw . . . one like the Son of man came with the clouds of heaven" (KJV). The imagery is rich—Jesus, the Son of Man, is ever-present and in the midst of Christians and the church. He is the unfailing Center.

John then goes on to tell his readers that the Son of man was dressed in a long, flowing robe cinched by a golden sash. This is descriptive of the garments worn by the Old Testament priests (Exodus 28:4), and the symbolism is used here to portray Christ as the great High Priest in God's new society, the church. It depicts divine dignity and authority.

Next we're told that the "hairs of his head were white, like white wool, like snow. His eyes were like a flame of fire" (1:14, ESV). God as the Ancient of Days is described this way in Daniel 7:9. In the Middle East, toward the end of the first century, white hair commanded respect as the sign of wisdom in years. John used this imagery here to represent Christ's purity and holiness and to portray Him as a wise ruler and judge. The reference to His eyes being "like a flame of fire" echoes Daniel 10:6 ("eyes were like flaming torches" [NASB]) and points to His role as a judge who penetrates the hidden depths of our hearts to encourage the faithful and bring judgment on the disobedient.

Again John employs Old Testament imagery when he speaks of Christ's feet as being like "burnished bronze" that glowed as if it had been "heated to a glow in a furnace" (1:15, NASB). This description has its origins in Daniel 10:6 and Ezekiel 1:13, 27, and 8:2. Here we have a picture of Christ's enduring strength and of His power. The last part of verse 15 says that His voice was like "the sound of many waters." When He speaks, it is with authority. And we catch this authority whether it comes in a Niagara-like roar or in the gentle, quiet flow of a slow-moving stream.

The vision draws to a close as John sees seven stars in Jesus's right hand—the people of God sheltered and protected by His right hand. He sees a two-edged sword, the Word of God, our source of protection and help. And, finally, John sees that "His face was like the sun shining in its strength" (1:16, NASB).

This magnificent word picture of the triumphant Christ dominates the rest of the book of Revelation. John wanted his readers of all time to have this picture firmly fixed in their minds before reading the rest of what he had to say. Political leaders like Emperor Domitian or a Stalin or a Hitler may have power and rule for a time—evil may seem to be in complete control—but Jesus Christ will always have the last word.

### What Was John's Reaction to the Vision?

"I fell at his feet as though dead" (1:17, NIV). John's response to what he sees is reverential awe and fear. But immediately he is told, "Fear not, I am the first and the last, and the living one. I died, and behold I am alive forevermore, and I have the keys of Death and Hades" (1:17–18, ESV).

In these words we have the assurance that there is no need to fear because He is divine—"the first and the last"; because He has been raised from the dead and is "alive forevermore": and because He has the power over our ultimate enemies, "Death and Hades."

And with that, John receives his instructions: "Write therefore the things that you have seen, those that are and those that are to take place after this" (1:19, ESV).

### The Letters to the Seven Churches (2:1–3:22)

While there were other churches in the province of Asia, John is told to write to seven of them. But as we mentioned earlier, seven is the number symbolizing completeness. Thus the "seven churches" are typical of *all* churches down through the centuries. Everyone was to read the entire book, not just the part of the letter addressed to a specific congregation.

The letters begin with the church at Ephesus on the Asian coast and follow the natural travel circuit of that day until finally arriving at Laodicea. Each of the letters has a common format. First, some quality of Christ drawn from the portrait of Him in Revelation chapter 1 is described because of its peculiar relevance to the individual church situation. Second comes either praise for a good record or reprimand for a bad one. Third, the church is given a promise of reward if it is victorious in the coming promise.

### The Church of Ephesus
John describes this church as being *magnificent in belief but stingy in love.*

If the mayor of Ephesus had bragged, "My city is the chief one in the province of Asia," he would have been right. It was a booming seaport, a gateway to the province, and on a main highway from the east to Rome. Ephesus was the home of the temple of Artemis, one of the seven wonders of the ancient world.

This is precisely why John addressed himself to this church first (2:1–7). It was an important church. Many years before, Paul, the apostle to the Gentiles, had worked there for at least three years. And now, as the One who holds the seven stars in His right hand and who walks in the middle of the seven golden lampstands begins to speak to this church, He compliments them on their work and patience, and He affirms them because they have not allowed false teachers and teachings to bespoil the church (2:2–3).

But then with penetrating directness, they are told that Christ has passed judgment on them because they "have forsaken the love [they] had at first"—they had lost their brotherly love (2:4, NIV). Yes, they still loved Christ, but they had come to hate anyone whose understanding of Christianity might be under question. Their opposition to heresy had given them an inquisitorial spirit that left no room for love; they were loyal but hateful. They had won the battle for truth and courage, but they had lost the war because they had forgotten that God is love.

This basic weakness of the church at Ephesus as it is illuminated in this part of our lesson has a sobering message for us today.

Our love for God is directly related to our love for others as expressed by the way we treat them. We can't truly love God and be racists or belligerent nationalists. We can't love God and be at odds with our Christian brothers and sisters and blind to their needs. Purity of doctrine is not an end in itself but is intended only as a means to lead us to trust, love, mercy, and justice. Truth is something to be done, to be acted on, not just believed.

Yes, we are to reject false teaching, but of supreme importance is that we are to hold on to our first love, our *agape* (uh-GAH-peh) love, that puts others—their cares, their hurts, their needs—first. No doubt we've all had too many encounters with belligerent Christians. Some of them claim to "hate the sin but love the sinner." But their treatment of "the sinner" makes a lie of that statement. In reality they will know we are Christians by our love. This is what the Ephesian Christians had forgotten.

### The Church in Smyrna

John describes this church as being *a poor little rich church.* The mayor of Smyrna could have said, "Ephesus may be first in commerce, but we are first in size and beauty. Our population is two hundred thousand, and no city in Asia is more artistically laid out or has more majestic public buildings." And he would have been right.

The "crown" of Smyrna was the civic plaza on top of Mount Pagos, the city's acropolis. Running from east to west was the famous "golden street," anchored on one end by the temple to Zeus and on the other by the temple to Cybele, with temples to Apollo, Asclepius, and Aphrodite between them.

Smyrna, modern Izmir in western Turkey, was famous for its libraries, music, art, and devotion to culture. One of the world's greatest writers, Homer, was born there.

Smyrna, like many centers in Asia Minor, was a dangerous place to be a Christian. It had long been a center of emperor worship, but this pagan practice actually accelerated during the closing years of the first century. It continued to prosper until the middle of the third century when emperor worship became universal. To practice caesar worship, the only requirement was for a person to go to the temple of caesar once a year, burn a small pinch of incense, and say, "Caesar is lord." Then they could go their own way for the rest of the year and worship the god or gods of their choice.

In reality, though, emperor worship had powerful political implications. To refuse to declare that caesar was lord was traitorous. So when Christians refused, their lives were at stake.

This was illustrated vividly around sixty years after John wrote, when Polycarp, the aged Christian bishop of Smyrna, was burned alive because he refused to renounce his faith in Christ. His dying words are still an inspiration: "Eighty-six years have I served Christ, and He has never done me wrong. How can I blaspheme my King who saved me?"

There was no reprimand in John's word for Smyrna (2:8–11). Rather, they were reminded that Christ, "the first and the last, which was dead, and is alive" (2:8, KJV), was very much alive and in control of their destiny in spite of the evil and the persecution they were suffering. The message for them was one of encouragement, and they were not to fear trial or prison or tribulation of any kind, because it wouldn't last long—ten days, symbolic of a short period of time. They were not even to fear death because death wasn't the greatest evil. But if they remained faithful and did suffer physical death, they were assured of "the crown of life" (2:10, ESV)—life with Christ throughout all the eternities ahead.

Smyrna suffered economic pressures and was a poor church in a prosperous city. Their sufferings were brought on by a certain faction of unbelieving and hostile Jews who used malicious slander, or "blasphemy" as some translations call it, to stir up persecution of the impoverished Christians. John words it this way in his message as Christ says, "I know your afflictions and your poverty—yet you are rich! I know about the slander of those who say they are Jews and are not, but are a synagogue of Satan" (2:9, NIV). It is possible that mob violence and looting had already stripped the Christians of their property.

The reference, though, to the synagogue of Satan makes it clear that it is Satan who is behind all of their suffering— wicked men were only his instruments. The reality of Satan and of the power of evil is clearly seen in these verses, but so is the promise of triumph for the believer: "The one who overcomes will not be hurt by the second death" (2:11, NASB). This was the same idea Paul was trying to get across to his readers in Rome when he insisted that nothing could separate Christians from the love of Christ (Romans 8:38–39).

To twenty-first-century Christians in the Western world who know nothing about the difficulties experienced by these Christians in Smyrna, there may seem to be little here that is relevant to us. But whatever the form of difficulty or hardship we are called to experience, we can learn much from our spiritual ancestors in the coastal city of Smyrna. We will do well to model their faithfulness. We, too, can listen to the One "who holds the seven stars in His right hand, the One who walks among the seven golden lampstands" (2:1, NASB) and not fear any of the emotional or physical difficulties that come our way as we attempt to live for the Lord in our community.

### The Church in Pergamos

This was *the too tolerant church* (2:12–17). The mayor of Pergamos, or Pergamum, could have quite truthfully claimed that his city was the most "religious" in all of the province of Asia. At the time John wrote this, Pergamos had become the provincial capital and was the center of emperor worship in the Roman world with three temples devoted to the caesar cult.

In fact, Pergamos was famous for its wide assortment of pagan temples. It was here in 29 BC that the first temple was built for worship of the Roman emperor. Pergamos was also noted for its medical center. Situated some forty-five miles north of Smyrna, it was a city of wealth and beauty. Its library, second only to the famous library in Alexandria, Egypt, contained two hundred thousand volumes. The city was also well known for its vellum or parchment factories that produced writing materials made from animal skins.

In verse 12 Christ identifies Himself as being the One "who has the sharp two-edged sword" (NIV). This was indeed a play on words that John's readers would have recognized because Rome had given this city the rare authority to carry out capital punishment, which was symbolized by the two-edged sword. But here Christ is reminding those Christians that He alone has the ultimate authority, not Emperor Domitian or imperial Rome.

The next words for the Christians in Pergamos were complimentary as Christ praises them for their faithfulness in the midst of intense persecution. He recognizes that they are Christians in a hostile city "where Satan's throne is" (2:13, NASB), the center for pagan and idolatrous worship. He then refers to Antipas, a faithful church member who had already been executed for his faith, for refusing to worship the statue of caesar (2:13). Tertullian, an early church leader, recorded that Antipas was boiled alive in oil.

But next, Christians in the church at Pergamos were told of their basic weakness. If Ephesus was the intolerant church, the church at Pergamos was too tolerant. False teachers were evidently allowed to circulate freely, luring some of the Christians to idolatry and immorality. These false teachers are compared to Balaam (Numbers 22; 31:16), who devised a deceptive plan to seduce the Israelite men (Revelation 2:14).

The reference in verse 14 is likely associated with some people inside the church who were teaching that it was all right to participate in the sacrificial meal of the pagan gods— "to eat things sacrificed to idols"—and to engage in sexual intercourse with the temple priestesses—"commit sexual immorality" (NASB).

In their desire to be accepted and influential in the community, apparently some in the church had decided to play the game with their pagan neighbors. After all, they may have reasoned, joining in some of the fun on Roman holidays surely wouldn't be too bad! But their leniency would lead to their ruin. Hence the warning, "Therefore repent. If not, I will come to you soon and war against them with the sword of my mouth" (2:16, ESV).

Next, the members of the Pergamos church who were compromising were told that if they would hear the word of the Lord and repent, healing would take place. "Hidden manna" from heaven would replace the illicit banquet food they had been eating in the pagan temples. White stones were frequently used as entry tickets to pagan banquets in Pergamos, and now Christ says here that He will give the faithful a white entry stone for His heavenly banquet. And their name on the stone will be a new one symbolic of their new life in Christ.

Yes, this picture language is rich in symbolism unfamiliar to us even though it was well-known to those first readers. Yet these words to that ancient Asian church have an immediate application to us. As servants of Christ we dare not compromise with the false gods of our twenty-first-century culture. To worship at the altar of power, money, political ambition, vocational success, sex, social acceptance, or personal popularity will cause us to lose our identity as children of the true God. Even to do good things for the wrong reasons is deadening compromise.

## The Church in Thyatira

The people to whom this communication is addressed could be called *the onward-and-upward church approaching the brink of expedience* (2:18–29). The mayor of Thyatira could easily have written something like this in the city's Chamber of Commerce brochure: "We are the commerce capital of Asia Minor. We manufacture more trade goods here than any other city in Asia Minor."

And that would have been right. This city, located about thirty miles from Pergamos on the banks of the Lycus River, was the trade union center of Asia Minor. Thyatira was a bustling trade center that had wool workers, clothing makers, dyers of purple cloth, tanners of leather, potters, bakers, bronzesmiths, and slave traders. It is likely the trade unions dominated the life of the city, and each union had its own patron god to whom they gave regular feasts that included sexual revelries.

Since Christians couldn't succeed in business without belonging to a trade union and participating in union events, they were put in a place of severe temptation just to earn a living. To refuse to participate could cost them their livelihood and subject them to intense persecution.

We learn in this part of our lesson that the church at Thyatira was outstanding. The "Son of God, who has eyes like a flame of fire" (2:18, NASB) recognized their steady progress toward spiritual maturity (2:18-19). He praises them for their love, service, and faithfulness.

But in spite of all that, this church had a serious flaw. They had allowed a false prophetess to remain in the church even though she favored sexual immorality and participation in pagan eating habits. This "Jezebel, who calls herself a prophetess" (2:20, NASB) was leading some believers to abandon their exclusive loyalty to Christ.

Evidently, this "Jezebel" had been duly warned but had refused to repent and change her ways. So in colorful picture language, judgment is pronounced against her sin (2:21-23). But happily, there were those in the church who saw through her false teaching, "Satan's so-called deep secrets" (2:24, NIV) —a teaching that indicated that the only way to overcome Satan was to learn all about sin through firsthand experience. Apparently, she had been teaching the deceptive notion that if you don't sin, you can't understand and appreciate grace. The idea was that you could be a better Christian if you'd really practiced what you had been saved from.

We would do well to take as our model this discriminating group in Thyatira that resisted this subtle false teaching.

They refused to let the demands of job or vocation dilute their Christian testimony. They were not ready to stoop to expediency for personal gain. And so in verses 26 through 28, those who are faithful—"the one who keeps My deeds until the end" (NASB)—are assured, again in colorful language, that God will reward them.

In all of this, we catch the importance of being faithful to Christ in the marketplaces of life. If we are to be effective witnesses of Jesus Christ, our work habits should be above reproach. We should be on time and not rob our employers by "goofing off." Our employers and our customers should receive full value from what we do. If we are to influence others for the Lord, our actions during every workday should be honorable, honest, and above reproach in every way.

### The Church in Sardis

A sign positioned above this first-century church could well have read, *The Duped, Declining, and Spiritually Dead Church,* and it was (3:1–6). In fact, we read, "And to the angel of the church in Sardis write: 'The words of him who has the seven spirits of God and the seven stars. "I know your works. You have the reputation of being alive, *but you are dead*"'" (3:1, ESV, italics added).

If someone had asked that late first-century mayor of Sardis, "Tell me three things that make your city notable," what would he have said?

"Well, first, we have the most impressive cemetery in all the province of Asia. It has so many burial mounds that we call it 'the place of a thousand hills.'

"Second, we have a great wool-dyeing industry; our white garments are famous and sell throughout the Roman Empire.

"Third, our city is located on a plateau fifteen hundred feet above sea level, and this makes it an ideal location to defend in time of war. The upper part of our city sits at eight hundred feet on the top of an acropolis that has a commanding view of the highways from Ephesus, Smyrna, Pergamos, and inland Asia Minor. This upper part of the city is impregnable.

"We are an ancient city with a famous past. Yes, it is true that we are suffering some decline, but this is a lovely and peaceful place to live."

"But, Mr. Mayor, haven't I read somewhere that in spite of your location, this 'impregnable' city has been conquered by enemy armies?"

"Well, yes. Twice we were taken completely by surprise. Cyrus the Persian conquered Sardis [in 549 BC] when, through our carelessness, he discovered a secret access to our fortress. And a similar thing happened [in 218 BC] when Antiochus the Great took our city."

Our fictional mayor was right—the city was in decline, and it would never recover. It was indeed dead, and until archaeologists began working there early in the twentieth century, it was nothing but a desolate and bleak place with a few scattered ruins.

Like the city, the first-century church at Sardis was dying too. A church that had once shown a vigorous loyalty to Christ had apparently compromised with the city's pagan society. It may have been at peace with the city, but it was spiritually dead, as dead as the graveyard a few miles away.

Inoffensive, harmless Christianity isn't real; it may be outwardly alive but inwardly dead.

But even under the dismal conditions described in our lesson, there was a ray of hope. There were apparently a few faithful Christians left in the city: "Yet you have still a few names in Sardis, people who have not soiled their garments" (3:4, ESV). And these were told to "wake up! Strengthen what remains and is about to die" (3:2, NIV).

For the faithful, Christ says "they shall walk with me in white: for they are worthy" (3:4, KJV). "The one who overcomes will be clothed . . . in white garments; and I will not erase his name from the book of life" (3:5, NASB). In other words, those Christians in the Sardis church who have retained their inner purity and haven't compromised their faith are assured of a lasting relationship with the Lord. Their citizenship is in heaven.

There was a moral minority in Sardis that serves as a model for us. While persecution still exists today, most of us are not threatened with persecution because we're Christians. Instead, the greatest danger to our spiritual vitality is in being too comfortable, of so blending into the "secular" lifestyle of society that most people we meet don't even know we are Christians.

But we, too, "will be clothed . . . in white garments" as we in our towns and cities love God and our neighbors—even our "enemies"—in the give-and-take of our daily lives. May the Spirit of Christ determine our actions behind the closed doors of our homes, in offices and shops, in the schoolroom, and even behind the wheel of our automobiles. Yes, on the surface as Christians we may feel outnumbered, but with Christ, we are the majority!

### *The Church in Philadelphia*
This could properly be labeled the missionary church that kept the faith (3:7–13).

Philadelphia was an important fortress city situated on the Roman road that linked it with Sardis, Pergamos, and Troas on the western coast. It was located twenty-five miles southeast of Sardis and one hundred miles east of Smyrna.

Philadelphia was founded around 150 BC by the Pergamenian King Attabus, who gave the city its name (which means brotherly love) out of loyalty to his own brother. If we had asked the mayor who was in office at the time John was writing why his city had been founded, he would likely have said, "Philadelphia is a missionary city. We were founded to bring Greek culture to the barbarians. Our city is on the western frontier of vast central Asia Minor and is of great influence."

It is likely that the Christian church in Philadelphia was the strongest of the seven. It is referred to in our lesson as the church of "an open door"—a strong missionary church. It saw itself as being located at the gateway of a great opportunity. The Christians there dared to dream the "impossible" dream of sharing the Good News with the whole Roman Empire.

It is apparent that this church faced opposition from "those who are of the synagogue of Satan, who claim to be Jews though they are not, but are liars" (3:9, NIV). This is evidently a reference to a group of Jews in the city who denied that Christ was the Messiah, and feeling ran high between them and the Christians. But in verse 10 these faithful Christians were assured of God's presence and keeping power.

As a final word of assurance to these Christians, the Lord reminds them that He will come again, and they are urged to hold steady to their faith (3:11) and are assured that in doing so they will become "a pillar in the temple of my God" (3:12, KJV). In other words, they would occupy a firm and unshakable place in Christ's new society, the eternal fellowship of faithful Christians.

Once again, this picture language is a bit obscure to us, but the Lord's assurance here and the wording used would have carried great meaning to the Philadelphia Christians. The city was evidently very close to an earthquake fault, and in AD 17 a disastrous quake had struck and leveled this Greek cultural center. Tacitus, the learned Roman historian (AD c. 55–c. 120), wrote in his *Annals* (Book II, #47), "That same year twelve famous cities of Asia fell by an earthquake in the night, so that the destruction was all the more unforeseen and fearful. Nor were there the means of escape usual in such a disaster, by rushing out into the open country, for there people were swallowed up by the yawning earth. Vast mountains, it is said, collapsed; what had been level ground seemed to be raised aloft, and fires blazed out amid the ruin. The calamity fell most fatally on the inhabitants of Sardis, and it attracted to them the largest share of sympathy."[1]

---

[1]Alfred John Church, William Brodribb, and Sara Bryant, eds. for *Perseus, Complete Works of Tacitus*. New York: Random House, Inc., reprinted 1942.

John's readers would be very familiar with the instability of their buildings and temples. But they were being assured here of the security of their position as "pillars" in God's temple. Then came a second promise to them as faithful Christians: "I will write on him the name of My God" (3:12, NASB). It was a custom in Philadelphia that a hero was sometimes honored by having a special pillar in one of the temples inscribed with his name.

What a powerful word of affirmation for the Philadelphia Christians! In spite of everything else that happens, they are assured of the stability of their position in Christ and will be "heroes" in God's fellowship of believers.

Philadelphia, the city of brotherly love in Asia, is our model for evangelism and Christian witnessing. Our commitment as believers in the Lord is to be witnesses daily in word and action of the richness of the Christian way of life. And our witness is to be spoken and lived out to our neighbors across the street and across the world.

Furthermore, we are never to be discouraged in our witnessing but can take heart in the possibility of unexpected results. The Philadelphia Christians were told that even some of their "enemies"—those of the "synagogue of Satan" (3:9, NASB)—might ultimately come to the Lord. We are to avoid limiting the Holy Spirit by assuming that some people are impossible.

### The Church in Laodicea

We'll call this *the rich little poor church*. It was an affluent church, the wealthiest of the seven, but it was also the weakest (3:14–22).

It was comfortable with the world because it had made peace with the world's values. It was lukewarm, "neither cold nor hot" (3:15, NIV).

The mayor of Laodicea in John's day would have undoubtedly been a person of wealth. He might have said, "There are more millionaires here per square yard than any city I know. When we were struck by our last earthquake [in AD 60], we refused government aid and rebuilt the city ourselves.

"We are a banking and textile center, and we have a famous medical school. We've become a leading financial center in Asia Minor. We've learned to compromise and accommodate ourselves to anyone.

"The only drawback to Laodicea is our poor water supply. Our water comes from ninety-five-degree hot springs located six miles south of the city and is brought here by way of aqueducts. By the time it gets here it is still distastefully warm."

Because of the large Jewish population in Laodicea, Christ identifies Himself in this message as "the Amen, the trusted and faithful and true Witness, the Beginning and Origin of God's creation" (3:14, AMP). This would have had great significance, especially to Jewish readers. In Hebrew the word *amen* literally means "foundation" and is, therefore, "faithful and true" (ESV). For the Jew, the reference point for foundation is the beginning in Genesis 1:1. Indeed, the message here is that Christ was the "Amen," the beginning point, the foundation on which everything rests.

Next, Christ accuses those Laodicean church people of being lukewarm just like their water supply. Instead of being lukewarm Christians, Christ wanted them to be boiling hot—enthusiastic, energetic, alive. Neutrality, compromise, complacency, self-satisfaction, and indifference are anti-Christian and useless to the Lord.

Because of their self-satisfaction, this denunciation probably came as a surprise to the Laodiceans, for they saw themselves as rich and in need of nothing (3:17). But the Lord tells them that in truth they are "wretched, pitiful, poor, blind and naked" (NIV). The spirit of the city had crept into their church and their spiritual life was paralyzed.

But the invitation to repent and change is always there, as Christ now says, "Behold, I stand at the door and knock. If anyone hears my voice and opens the door, I will come in to him and eat with him, and he with me" (3:20, ESV). Here is the grand invitation and promise that has thrilled Christians of every century. As we open ourselves up to Jesus Christ, we have a relationship with Him of a most intimate kind. He never forces the door open, but as we open ourselves to Him, He responds immediately.

The Laodicean letter ends with a note of joy (3:21). On Calvary, Christ overcame all forms of evil. Golgotha was not a defeat but a victory, and Christians of all time are invited to share in that eternal victory with the Lord.

### A Concluding Word

In reading these special communications to the seven churches, we are reminded that the recipients of this letter were real people in real places. John knew them and their cities well and frequently used word pictures that aligned with the specific church's culture and surroundings. He was writing to these people, but we can see that in each case important things have been said that apply to us and to our church life.

While the language is picturesque, and the first-century images used are frequently vague or unfamiliar to us today, Christ is speaking to us here in the twenty-first century in an intensely practical way. There are words of both warning and encouragement for us.

*Dear Lord, thank You for the privilege of learning about You. I am grateful for the special fellowship I have with You— learning of You, learning from You, loving You. AMEN.*

# PATMOS

John, the writer of the book of Revelation, was an exiled prisoner of the Roman government at the time he received the visions described in the book of Revelation. He was held on the island of Patmos. It is one of the Sporades Islands located in the Aegean Sea, roughly twenty-eight miles off the coast of Asia Minor—modern Turkey—but is now part of Greece. Its residents are known as Patmians. The island is about eight miles long by six miles at its widest point. Many Christians make pilgrimages to Patmos to visit the Cave of the Apocalypse, traditionally held to be the site where John experienced his visions, as well as the Monastery of St. John the Theologian. In 2009 *Forbes* named Patmos "Europe's most idyllic place to live."

# *Notes*

# Notes

# The Heart of John's Message

*Lord God, open my understanding as I study Your Word, and help me to bring Your Word into my day-to-day living.* AMEN.

The scriptures for this lesson, chapters 4 and 5, form the theological heart of the book of Revelation. These chapters forthrightly address the two problem situations that absorb John's attention: the internal threat of false beliefs or heresy, and the external threat of state persecution.

In chapter 4, John paints a colorful and sublime picture of God as the Creator of the universe. This was to help guide the churches to deal with and solve the internal problem of false teaching and false belief, particularly a belief that was being taught by a group of church members whom John identifies as Nicolaitans (2:6). Apparently these people confused liberty with license, accepting the idea that because the body is intrinsically evil, there is no reason people can't do what they please with it. This, of course, led to both moral and spiritual compromise and degradation.

Then, in chapter 5, John addresses the external problem—that of confronting Emperor Domitian's persecution and threat of extermination. This cold-blooded madman was determined to rid the empire of all "atheists"—those who did not worship the pagan gods and who refused to call him "lord and god." Christians and Jews were especially singled out for his most barbarous acts of persecution.

It was John's belief that if he could get the churches to purify their teaching from the heresies that attacked from within, they would be strong enough to confront the external holocaust propagated by Rome. In effect, John is saying here that the "One who made us is the same One who saves us." He is more powerful than any of the world's power structures. To hold steady and be strong, Christians must worship God as both Creator and Redeemer.

## The Throne of God (4:1–7)

### *God in Heaven*

In chapter 1 of Revelation, John gave us a vision of the victorious Christ who had risen from the tomb in a blaze of victory. Then in chapters 2 and 3, John gave us an earthly picture of the risen Christ as He "moved" among the seven churches. Now, though, the scene shifts from earth to heaven as John writes, "After this I looked, and there before me was a door standing open in heaven. And the voice I had first heard speaking to me like a trumpet said, 'Come up here, and I will show you what must take place after this'" (4:1, NIV).

As would be expected, the wording here reflects the ancient view of the universe—heaven was "up." It was a vault "above" the earth where God lived. The earth, the home of the human race, was "below" heaven. "Below" the earth was Sheol or Hades—the underworld where the departed dead were confined. And so it is natural that John, in writing to those first-century Christians, would use this three-storied-world idea in taking us up into

God's throne room. From now on in our studies of Revelation, we will frequently move between heaven and earth. As we shall see, what happens on earth has its counterpart in heaven.

## *"A Door Was Opened"*

John begins his description by saying that he saw "a door standing open in heaven" (4:1, NIV) and was allowed to look in. Our human understanding can't grasp the idea or the reality of heaven, for it is a spiritual location for us now. But it is where God lives; it is the place where all the masks are off and where good and evil are seen for what they really are.

Next, John says he heard a voice that had the sound of a trumpet. Again, we have the image of the trumpet symbolizing the voice of Christ. This symbol first appeared in verse 10 of chapter 1. And from Christ came the great invitation: "Come up here, and I will show you what must take place after this" (4:1, NIV). Under the influence of the Spirit, the vision unfolded as John looked and moved through the open door.

What John saw was so dramatic and so utterly breathtaking that it takes two whole chapters for him to describe it. Through the open door John saw the throne room of heaven. What a startling scene—this was the seat of God's rule, the place of action.

We're always at a loss when it comes to describing the things of God in human language. But that's all we have to work with, so we have to do the best we can while always remembering that our very words are only symbols we use in an inept attempt to describe the indescribable.

For our purposes we might compare the throne room of God with the World War II "war room" of Prime Minister Winston Churchill. In that war room were battle maps marked with flags to show the location of the battles and the army units that were poised to crush Hitler's armies.

Like Churchill's maps and flags, John's vision revealed a heavenly map of God's war against evil. What John saw as he looked into that throne room is described with Old Testament and apocalyptic images and symbols that are quite foreign to us but that would have been immediately recognized and appreciated by his first-century readers. Twenty-first-century readers may find the picture is unintelligible unless we get some sort of understanding of the code.

### A Throne Set in Heaven

The throne was the first thing John saw in his vision. It symbolized God's presence and power, His majesty and sovereignty. What an awesome and encouraging image to those desperate, disheartened, and persecuted first readers!

God's awesome presence on the throne is central to everything else around Him. But John is obviously reluctant to use any human characteristic to describe Him. Of course we can't see God's form on the throne, although the vision is full of movement and sound and color. God is too bright for us to look at Him, but He illuminates everything around Him. Even as we can't stare into the sun but we see its brilliance all around us, so it is that while we can't see God directly, we see Him in all that He lights up. No, John's outer vision could in no way describe God, but he could see and feel the majesty, mercy, glory, purity, and power of God.

### Descriptive Symbols

"And He who was sitting was like a jasper stone and a sardius in appearance; and there was a rainbow around the throne, like an emerald in appearance" (4:3, NASB). This description is rich in Old Testament imagery. The brilliant jasper and the red sardius stone remind us of the high priest's breastplate (Exodus 28:17–21), and they quite likely symbolize God's transcendent majesty and righteousness, resulting in judgment against sin.

The circular, halo-like rainbow "like an emerald" is reminiscent of the bow in the cloud God first showed to Noah (Genesis 9:16). It, too, represented God's promises, which signified life and hope to the persecuted Christians.

And in verse 4, John says that "surrounding the throne were twenty-four other thrones, and seated on them were twenty-four elders. They were dressed in white and had crowns of gold on their heads" (4:4, NIV). There are various explanations for these twenty-four elders, but many Bible scholars believe they represent all of redeemed humanity— the saints of the Old Testament and the Christians of all time. These are the "old Israel" and the "renewed Israel." The white robes suggest righteousness and spiritual purity, and the crowns may well symbolize victory and faithfulness. What an unbelievably glorious and breathtaking sight!

But that isn't all. "And out of the throne proceeded lightnings and thunderings and voices: and there were seven lamps of fire burning before the throne, which are the seven

Spirits of God. And before the throne there was a sea of glass like unto crystal" (4:5–6, KJV). Again, we are reminded of Old Testament imagery, for in the lightning, voices, and thunder we catch a picture of Mount Sinai as God revealed Himself at the giving of the Law (Exodus 19:16).

The "seven lamps of fire" are symbolic of the Holy Spirit, for throughout the Bible fire symbolizes the Spirit of God. Father, Son, and Holy Spirit are all represented in this awesome scene.

Then apparently a flat, pavement-like surface (probably semiprecious stones) was located between John and the throne. It looked like a "sea of glass, like crystal" (4:6, NASB). The thrones of ancient kings often rested on such surfaces to highlight the monarch's importance and to symbolize the distance between royalty and ordinary people.

This splendid vision of God's awesome presence becomes strange and unsettling when John next writes, "And round about the throne, were four beasts full of eyes before and behind [in front and back]" (4:6, KJV). These four strange animals probably represent all of living creation. There is an interesting similarity between this description and the one in Ezekiel 1:10.

Who and what are these strange creatures? There are, of course, various explanations, but it is likely they point to the natural division of living things as they were cataloged in John's day: (1) the lion symbolizes wild animals; (2) the ox represents domestic animals; (3) man is symbolic of the human race; and (4) the eagle symbolizes all birds. The meaning of this magnificent picture comes through as a powerful truth: all creation praises God the Creator!

Yes, John dipped his paintbrush in Ezekiel's paint pot, but this talented and poetic man is wonderfully imaginative and creative in his understanding and use of these creatures. The term "full of eyes" gives the impression of their all-encompassing knowledge of God, and the "six wings" symbolize their unlimited mobility in doing God's will (4:8a).

The individual elements of John's vision may baffle us, but we need to be able to see the larger picture. Imagine that you're making a long-anticipated visit to Arizona's Grand Canyon. Like most people, you'd take a large number of photos to share with your friends on social media. But not even a thousand pictures can do justice to that great panorama of nature. There is just no way the grandeur of the canyon can be captured by even the finest camera lens.

And there is no way we can capture the grandeur of John's grand and complex vision through individual glimpses. We need the larger view, and this will begin to come clear to us as we look closely now at the five great hymns found next in our scripture lesson. It is in these hymns that the central message of John's vision can be found. They are indeed the most important part of this grand event.

## The First Two Hymns (4:8-11)

"Holy, holy, holy, is the Lord God Almighty, who was and is and is to come!" (4:8, ESV). As heaven breaks out with the sound of music, we catch a bit of a parallel between this and the magnificent Sanctus of Isaiah: "Holy, holy, holy is the Lord of hosts; the whole earth is full of his glory!" (Isaiah 6:3, ESV).

## The First Hymn

With the Emperor Domitian taking God's name in vain, those readers in the seven churches must have been lifted off their seats with this magnificent affirmation of God's holiness. At the same time, they were reassured by the word that the God who is the all-powerful and righteous force of the entire universe is also the One who influences the destiny of the entire human race.

This first hymn also gives living testimony that the true and righteous God of history is eternal—"who was and is and is to come!" "Little tin gods" like Emperor Domitian at the end of the first century and Adolf Hitler in the twentieth century are temporary evil geniuses, but they soon pass from the scene.

But the "Holy One" is over and above and beyond His creation. He has all power and presence from eternity to eternity, and that power is always used for good. Yes, there is only one God, and that God *is not Caesar.*

The awe-filled thinking expressed in this first hymn is one that seems to be neglected in many churches today. The Bible teacher Dr. J. B. Phillips wrote, "Our God is too small." We've made Him friendly and loving, and that is right and true. But at the same time, we've lost the sense of His holiness, and that is often reflected in the tone of our worship. To grasp John's vision at this point is to participate in the mystery of all creation's praise for the Creator as it is expressed in the 148th Psalm.

## The Second Hymn

"Worthy are You, our Lord and our God, to receive glory and honor and power; for You created all things, and because of Your will they existed, and were created" (4:11, NASB). This second hymn shows the twenty-four elders—all of God's people—worshipping and praising the holy God, their Creator.

In this hymn the twenty-four elders acknowledge that God in His gracious love has created and surrounded us with the marvelous world of sensations, sounds, and colors. Everything that exists originated with Him. They acknowledge that He continues to show His love for us by renewing the world daily. He has never been and never will be an absentee landlord who stands aloof from His creation. We're not alone in this universe of God's making, and the day will come when we will be a part of His new heaven and new earth.

This second hymn sets the book of Revelation squarely in opposition to Greek thought about origins and meanings. The hymn asserts emphatically that the God of Jesus Christ is the Originator of everything that exists. This, of course, is sound teaching, both from the viewpoint of the Old Testament (Genesis 1) and the New (John 1). Religion has a practical, earthy implication.

But the Greek thinkers viewed the origin of things from an entirely different perspective. And it was this Greek concept that had stained the thinking of some of the Christians at Pergamum, Ephesus, and Thyatira. This particular Greek heresy is what we refer to as Gnosticism. It will help us to better understand why John wrote as he did in chapter 4 if we briefly review this heresy.

The Greeks, following the thinking of the great philosopher Plato, were suspicious of the created world with all its concrete, sweaty reality where we live out the daily twenty-four-hour cycles of our physical lives. They believed there were two worlds: the world of spirit where God, or the gods, live in holy purity, and the world of matter, where we live, that is evil and corrupt. They taught that a bad deity had created the world out of evil and existing matter. From the very beginning the world was imperfect.

Gnostic thought centered on the idea that because God would have nothing to do with the evil material world, salvation was only attainable as a person escaped to the world of spirit where God lived. On the other hand, a Demiurge—the evil spiritual being who had created the physical world—was jealously guarding every exit to prevent people from escaping.

The Gnostics claimed that they were the only ones who had the secret of getting us out of the prison of matter and into the world of the spirit. They also believed their "special knowledge" could be used to fan the "divine spark" within other believers and they would then come to know the good God who lived in His spiritual world. There were those who insisted this new state could best be achieved through a rigorous, ascetic rejection of the world and even of their physical bodies.

But the bolder and more extremist Gnostics believed they had already been released from all material ties, including decency and morality, and so it really didn't matter what they did with their physical bodies because they had nothing to do with their spiritual state. It was this group of undisciplined Nicolaitans who were polluting the Asian churches that John spoke against in this fourth chapter. John was determined to vigorously oppose this unhealthy worldview that was diametrically at odds with the truth as it is found in Scripture.

The Gnostic believers in the churches saw these words of John as a direct assault on their system. Here he is saying that creation is good because God is good. The world is "well done" because God made it; Domitian might be turning the world into a perverse, bad joke, but his days are numbered. John wanted his readers to see and understand without question that God was the Creator. He knew that they would then be prepared to accept Him fully as the Lord of life. With that firmly settled in their minds and hearts they would be better equipped to weather the storm of persecution that was threatening them.

But this second hymn speaks to us today as well with compelling force. It affirms and gives us confidence in our beginnings. As Christians we can hold our heads high as a creation of God, and we can accept our bodies in spite of our weaknesses and limitations.

Then, too, as children of God we are reminded through this hymn of our sacred responsibility to care deeply about every part of God's creation—our fellow human beings wherever they are, and the magnificence of the world of nature around and above us. All of this is God's world, and He is still in control. And then, with that amazing truth firmly fixed in our minds, we can join with the vast heavenly throngs and sing praises to God.

Unfortunately, though, not all of John's early readers heeded his warning against the insidious heresy of Gnosticism. Only around fifty years after John wrote these words a churchman named Marcion firmly rejected the Old Testament God as an evil creator. He urged his followers to reject this God in favor of a "spiritual God" who could best become known through an asceticism and monasticism that rejected the material world. Fortunately, Marcion's folly attracted only a few because of the effects of the pure teachings of John on the early church.

## God the Redeemer (5:1–14)

We have just seen in chapter 4 of our scripture lesson the part of John's vision of God on His throne in which He is being praised by the hosts of heaven as the Creator of the universe. Now, as we move into chapter 5, the drama changes as we see God being worshipped and praised as the Redeemer of the world.

### *The Scroll with Seven Seals*

As John continues to watch the scene around God's heavenly throne, his attention is suddenly riveted on an object that was in His right hand (5:1–5). "Then I saw in the right hand of him who was seated on the throne a scroll written within and on the back, sealed with seven seals" (verse 1, ESV). Interestingly enough, John had previously hinted that God had no form, but there was no other way to tell his readers that God was holding a book than to speak of it as being in His hand.

In referring to the scroll that was in God's hand, John makes it clear that it was securely "sealed with seven seals." From this we get the picture that only God knew the contents. It was a first-century practice to place the personal seal of the owner on any important document. And while our scripture doesn't directly indicate what was in the scroll, from the content of the two hymns and what follows, it is likely safe for us to assume that it contained the vast record of world events from creation to the end times, along with an explanation of all it meant in God's plan for His creation.

Next John writes that he saw and heard an angel who asked, "Who is worthy to open the scroll and break its seals?" (5:2, ESV). We can easily imagine John's eagerness as he viewed this scene from his place of confinement on Patmos. The writing on that scroll spoke to his future, and he had to be anxious about what it said. Undoubtedly his first readers had this same sense of anticipation in the midst of their own extremely difficult times of persecution.

What did the future hold for them? was the question. Would the powers in Rome ease their persecution of the Christians? Would mad Emperor Domitian increase his fury and send them to their deaths in an arena? Would God over-rule the powers of evil that seemed to be shaking the world like a rabid dog? Yes, the angel's question was important to John as he viewed this strange scene—and it would be later to his readers in the churches too.

But then comes the devastating word (5:3). No person anywhere—in heaven, on earth, or under the earth—steps forward to open the book to see what is written in it. No one is worthy. John's anticipation is drowned in a sea of despair, and he begins "to weep loudly" (5:4, ESV). The promise made at the beginning of this vision (4:1) that John and his readers would be shown the future couldn't be kept because no one was worthy to open the scroll.

But in the midst of his despair "one of the elders" comes forward to comfort him and give him the great good news: "the Lion of the tribe of Judah, the Root of David, has conquered, so that he can open the scroll and its seven seals" (5:5, ESV). This kingly Lion, of course, refers to the Messiah who was predicted in the Old Testament (Genesis 49:9–10; Isaiah 11:1–10). It was He who would rescue His people.

### The Lion-Lamb

When John turns back toward God's throne to see this Lion, he sees instead "a Lamb, looking as if it had been slain" (5:6–8, NIV). Instead of a roaring and conquering Lion, John sees the striking figure of a Lamb that had been killed but had triumphed over death and was alive again. And this Lamb is able to see John, the seven churches, and all of the world through the "seven eyes"— the Holy Spirit. Nothing is hidden from Him.

This new image of the Lion-Lamb brings together the Davidic Messiah of the Old Testament and the Suffering Servant (Isaiah 42–53).

In lesson 1 of this book we saw Christ portrayed as the Victor. Now we see how He won that victory—through His self-sacrifice. This served as a vivid reminder to John's first readers that Christ didn't win His battles in the conventional Roman way, with weapons of war and the exercise of political power. Instead, His victory came on Calvary's cross. And because of His victory there, we, too, can overcome the powers of evil.

As strange as this part of John's vision may seem to us, it has profound meaning. The Lion-Lamb, Jesus Christ, is the One worthy to open the scroll. He is the focal point of the Christian faith. It is only in Him that we find the meaning of life; He is the One who pulls everything in the universe together. It isn't the sword of Rome or of any world power since that day but the sword of the Spirit that wins out in the long run.

And like Christ, our Lion-Lamb, we gain life by losing our lives in Him—that is the Good News. This eternal truth has stood the test of centuries and of the experience of God's people throughout all time.

For those first-century readers in the seven churches of Asia, the Domitian way to victory stood in stark contrast to the Lamb. Only through "eyes of faith" could they see that the Lamb was the real winner. Emperor Domitian imposed his will and crushed people through power and violence. His evil power was the power to kill, and this he was doing with passion.

The power of the Lamb, on the other hand, never forces or brutalizes. It is expressed in self-giving. Jesus's death on the cross represents the failure of evil. And His resurrection liberates us from the idea that violence is a means that can be used to bring about God's will on the earth.

Through violence, the Domitians of this world have tried in vain to overcome all opposition, but Jesus and the people of God, as in the story of the Good Samaritan, find fulfillment in the giving of themselves—of their time and energy and money to relieve the suffering, the injured, the "have-nots" of the world. This is true power!

But let's go back to John's vision. John and his first readers must have been thrilled to understand that the Lamb, the Lord Jesus, could break the seals. He alone had the scroll of their future. They understood now that Christ controls the future, and He could make sense out of the scroll.

With this knowledge firmly embedded into their hearts and minds, those beleaguered first-century Christians now knew that their lives were in God's hands. Life and death took on an entirely new meaning for them. And for those of us who are carving out life some two thousand years later, the idea that we're not riding a world gone wild gives us confidence and boldness to confront the future. We know it isn't true that "[life] is a tale told by an idiot, full of sound and fury, signifying nothing," as Shakespeare's Macbeth declared. We don't buy into the idea that all we learn from history is that we learn nothing from it. Christ, the Lamb, has the last word; the book on the future is His.

Next, John writes in verse 8 that when Christ (the Lamb) took the scroll, the permanent attendants in the throne room stretched themselves out before Him in worship. And we learn that they used their harps as accompaniment for their "new song" (5:9, NIV). Then he adds that the heavenly choir held "golden bowls full of incense, which are the prayers of the saints" (5:8, ESV). The good news for those first readers and us is that our prayers are in God's presence. We have immediate access to God through Jesus Christ.

### The Third Hymn

This third hymn might well be titled "The Lamb as Redeemer" (5:9–10). This magnificent hymn focuses on some of the key aspects of Christ's ministry. First, praise is given because the Lamb that was slain has redeemed us. Christ willingly

surrendered His life on the cross for our sins, and through
that divine act we were brought into a proper relationship
with Him.

We learn next from this third hymn that Christ's redeeming
work was for everybody in all time—"every tribe, language,
people, and nation" (5:9, NASB). God's salvation knows no
time, racial, or national boundaries.

This hymn tells us, finally, that our all-encompassing,
worldwide Christian fellowship is a royal priesthood of
believers: "You have made them into a kingdom and priests
to our God, and they will reign upon the earth" (5:10, NASB).
We, together, are a royal priesthood. As sons and daughters of
the King, by virtue of our being priests, we have access to God
at all times. This was a whole new idea in the ancient world.

### The Fourth Hymn

All that has gone before is now followed with an explosion
of praise (5:11–12). Untold thousands of voices join in song,
"Worthy is the Lamb that was slain to receive power, and
riches, and wisdom, and strength, and honour, and glory, and
blessing" (KJV). What a vivid contrast this would have been
to those first readers. Jesus used the gifts of riches, power,
wisdom, strength, honor, and glory to lift up and help people,
while Emperor Domitian used his gifts to force other people
to help further his causes and ambitions.

### The Fifth Hymn

Finally, then, in a grand finale, the whole universe joins in
the singing of praise to God and to Christ for His victory

(5:13–14). All of nature joins in praise. What a grand affirmation of the greatness of our Lord!

What can one say in response to such holy grandeur? Only what the representatives of God's creation of animals, birds, and human beings could say at this point: "Amen!" (5:14, ESV). For me, Handel's *Messiah* with its ending chorus has caught the feeling of this throne room vision: the joy and shock of the mighty Lion becoming the little Lamb.

God was so secure in His love that He could come in humility as a little sheep and rescue us from our fear of the brutal and evil powers of the world. A glimpse into God's magnificent throne room makes the pomp and circumstance of the Domitians in all history seem like a shabby little sideshow.

The twentieth century saw its share of despots, dictators, and autocrats, such as Stalin, Hitler, Mussolini, Saddam Hussein, Pinochet, Franco, Mao, and Castro. The twenty-first century is following in its footsteps. But many of these have faded or are fading. However, the holiness and majesty of our God only grow more brilliant as we see and learn more of the wonders of His universe. These hymns assure us that the future need hold no fear for the children of God, for our Creator-Redeemer gives our future meaning and hope.

Amen.

*Heavenly Father, thank You for delivering me from the gnawing, paralyzing effects of fear. You have given me a spirit of power, of love, and of a sound mind. AMEN.*

# SARDIUS AND JASPER

John drew often on precious and semi-precious gemstones to tell his readers what heaven looked like. Two that stand out are jasper and sardius. John even uses them to describe the appearance of God: "He who was sitting [God] was like a jasper stone and a sardius in appearance" (Revelation 4:3, NASB). Both jasper and sardius are included among the twelve stones on the Israelite high priest's breastplate.

Jasper is an opaque stone that is a form of chalcedony. When it breaks, it breaks into smooth surfaces, which makes it ideal for polishing. It can take on many colors, though green, yellow, brown, and red are perhaps most common. It is associated with the Israelite tribe of Reuben.

Sardius, not surprisingly, shares a connection with one of the seven churches in Revelation: Sardis, the area from which these stones originate. A form of carnelian, sardius is associated with the tribe of Benjamin. It is most often a deep blood-red in hue, which comes from the presence of iron oxide. It is also known as sardian or sardine stone.

# Notes

_____

_____

_____

_____

_____

_____

_____

_____

_____

_____

_____

_____

_____

_____

_____

_____

_____

_____

_____

_____

_____

_____

_____

# *Notes*

# The Winners and the Losers in History

---

*Savior, thank You for making me a winner by doing all You've done for me. I win—in even the most losing circumstances—because of who You are.* AMEN.

I n our last lesson, John took us up to heaven and gave us a view through the open door of the throne room of God, the Creator-Redeemer. There we saw a remarkable vision of worship and music where the Lamb finally stepped forward to open the scroll of history and show what is in the future between the time of John's vision and the Second Coming of Christ.

Now in this lesson we have the beginning of John's promise to reveal the things soon to come to pass (1:1; 4:1). The Christians in the seven churches in the Roman province of Asia and the Christians of our century are eager to see what is going to happen.

Who will be the winner in this titanic struggle between good and evil in our world? Surely those first-century Christians wondered whether the winner then would be Domitian or Christ, even as the Christians in the 1940s wondered whether the powers of evil under Hitler and his

Axis cohorts would win, or whether the opposing forces in both the East and the West would be the overcomers.

John's answer in the book of Revelation to the first-century struggle is dramatically arranged in a series of symbolic events as the seven seals of the scroll of history are broken. Indeed, the apocalyptic writings that John's first readers would have known so well predicted a series of rampant evils to spoil the earth before history came to an end. These were wars, earthquakes, famine, persecution, and unusually violent activities in the sun, moon, and stars.

The apocalyptic writers had the genius to portray a crisis in a life-and-death way—to isolate and exaggerate in order to more clearly portray a truth. The twenty-first-century counterpart to all of this is the political cartoon or the meme. Often facial and bodily features are grossly exaggerated, as are gestures and actions. The editorial pages of our papers as well as the internet are plastered with this sort of cartoon, especially during election years.

Through images and the use of clever and colorful metaphor John does these same things with words. He has the rare gift of painting with broad strokes and helping us see things that we would have missed otherwise.

With a few bold strokes of his word-brush, John will show us that even though outwardly it appears the forces in this world are victorious, when he adds a few more strokes, we see them as defeated and gobbled up by a mass of apocalyptic horrors. Outwardly, the world looks like it was oriented toward life, but in reality it is aligned with death.

On the other hand, when John gives us his portrait of the church, it appears to be completely defeated. But then when he adds a few more strokes, we are able to see the church as the ultimate victor. At first glance, what seems to be the way it is with both the world and the church is actually quite different as John completes the picture—the winners are the losers, and the losers are really the winners.

This is indeed the great irony of history that is best portrayed in the apocalyptic form of literature. For those of us in the western world in the twenty-first century, all of this seems very obscure and ambiguous. As pragmatic literalists, we are pathetically unaccustomed to irony. And now here in our lesson we are confronted by the greatest irony of the cosmos—the Lord of the universe is indeed the Lamb that was crucified on Golgotha by Roman soldiers. It is good that John wrote his message here in the broad pictures of apocalyptic symbols. Otherwise we might well miss his subtle philosophy of history.

## The Four Horsemen of the Apocalypse (6:1-8)

John now turns the carousel of history, and we watch the horses go by, representing the basic forces of conquering or conquest, warfare, famine, and death. He saw these forces at work in the late first-century world as the Roman armies marched across and controlled the known world of that time. As we contemplate the movement of history since the first century, we can see these same "horses" galloping across the world, and we are still hearing their hoofbeats today.

The roots of John's vision may be found in the writing of the prophet Zechariah (1:8–11; 6:1–8). John saw in each of these four horses and their riders great destructive forces sent by God against an evil and chaotic world before the end of time as we know it.

### The White Horse of Conquest

The opening words of our scripture lesson might well read, "Now I watched when the Lamb opened one of the seven seals, and I heard one of the four living creatures say with a voice like thunder, 'Come!' And I looked, and behold, a white horse! And its rider had a bow, and a crown was given to him, and he came out conquering, and to conquer" (6:1–2, ESV). In the Old Testament, the bow symbolizes military might, and we have here a specter of violent tyranny and brutal military conquest.

It is interesting to note that it was the Persians who first introduced the horse to Palestine, and the Jews connected it primarily with war. Most certainly, the picture that would have come to John's first readers was that of returning victorious Roman generals who rode white horses in their victory parades at the end of a successful campaign.

The white horse stands for the abuse of political power that always brings pain and suffering to the world. Every period of time has suffered from these conquering heroes, from the time of Alexander the Great to the caesars, Napoleon, and Hitler. These *counterchrists* have been nothing more than false messiahs who have deliberately used political and military power to bring the masses under their control and force from them an adulation that bordered on worship. The salute "Heil Hitler" could readily be interpreted as "Hitler is our salvation."

You will recall during the time of Jesus's temptation in the wilderness following His baptism that Satan tried to lure Him to the use of political power as a shortcut to achieving His mission in the world. But Jesus knew that assertion of power wouldn't provide the answer to the deepest needs of people. He knew that a pattern of violence could not produce peace. Those who live by the sword will die by the sword. Those who use deceit in order to bring about the way of truth are eventually trapped in the web of their own falsehoods. Jesus certainly knew that there was no future in telling lies for the greater glory of God.

In their insecurity, the Roman emperors were constantly on the move in a frenetic effort to conquer and expand their influence. Undoubtedly, they would have thought, *We aren't greedy. We just want all of the world that adjoins ours.*

It has been estimated that toward the end of the first century there were about sixty-five million slaves in the Roman Empire. It was this vast network of human chattel that held together the workings of Roman society. Raw, conquering power was the only glue the emperors knew that could hold their world together. The white horse and rider in this lesson symbolized the brutal power of conquest.

### The Red Horse of War

The pride and greed of the white horse and rider inevitably brings on the bright red horse of war (6:3–4). John writes, "Its rider was permitted to take peace from the earth, so that people should slay one another, and he was given a great sword" (6:4, ESV).

The devastation of war, of men fighting against their fellow men, has been the world's pattern since earliest time. History is littered with the tragic debris of bloodshed, famine, and death as the red horse of war has ridden roughshod over human society. Unlike have battled with unlike; friends have turned on friends; brothers have fought with brothers, as the power-hungry caesars of every century have attempted to ransack and conquer the world.

Jesus warned us of this endless cycle when He said, "When you hear of wars and rumors of wars, do not be alarmed (frightened, troubled); these things must take place, but the end is not yet" (Mark 13:7, AMP).

Christians have always had to live with the white and red horses. A man who was a young boy during World War II remembered vividly his fear that his older brothers who were in the armed services would be killed and he would never see them again. Fear that the war would drag on until he, too, would have to go and face death. The terror of those days clutched at the hearts of millions of flesh-and-blood people and left an ugly scar on the world.

But the message of Jesus sounds a different note. As His followers, we are to be continuously involved in the seemingly endless task of peacemaking. As the "salt of the earth," we can't stand back and be trampled by either the white horse of conquest or the red horse of war. Even as Jesus in His time stood boldly against conquest and war, so must we be vigorous advocates of peace. But Christ's pattern for triumph was not that of the angry zealots of His day. Instead, His victory came through love and self-giving, and enduring hardship. He is our model for resistance.

## The Black Horse of Famine

The tragic story of history tells us that conquest leads to war and war leads to famine. When a country was ravaged by the Roman armies in the first century, there were food shortages, hunger, and starvation. This is still the pattern laid down by twenty-first-century armies whether war rages in Eastern Europe, Central America, Africa, or the Middle East.

John writes that the rider of the black horse carried "a pair of scales in his hand" (6:5, NASB). These symbolize an economy that has gotten out of balance because of conquest and war where the rich have not suffered but the poor are destitute and starving.

Then in verse 6 the voice says, "A quart of wheat for a denarius, and three quarts of barley for a denarius . . ." (ESV). The extent of the food shortage described here is critical. Enough wheat to feed one person would cost a full day's wages, and yet an entire family would have to subsist on this amount. On the other hand, it might be possible to feed a family on less-desirable barley. This is a picture of an intense food shortage.

John's first readers would have understood this picture of shortage and hunger that would precede the end of time as we know it. They had suffered excruciating food shortages and famine during Emperor Nero's reign, and at one point during Domitian's reign the shortage of grain had been acute.

On the other hand, the voice is describing a situation here that has plagued society from the earliest of time: while the poor suffered and got poorer, the rich got richer. This is the idea behind the closing words of verse 6, "and do not harm the oil and wine!" (ESV). These words point to the luxuries the rich were able to acquire, even during times of extreme shortage, through bribery and the black market. It is a sick society that makes it possible for the "haves" to live in comfort and luxury when a significant percentage of people in the world are hungry and starving to death.

The black horse of famine is still thundering across our world. The imprint of its hoofbeats is seen as our computer and television screens picture skin-and-bones people in Africa, India, and war-ravaged countries in the Middle East. We cringe at such sights and make token efforts. But Jesus's words are our indictment: Since you haven't helped them, you haven't helped Me. Somehow we as Christians need to see that the black horse of famine can and must be driven into oblivion.

### The Pale Horse of Death

With the opening of the fourth seal John writes, "And I looked, and behold a pale horse: and his name that sat on him was Death, and Hell followed with him. And power was given unto them over the fourth part of the earth, to kill with sword, and with hunger, and with death, and with the beasts of the earth" (6:8, KJV). This is a ghastly and sinister picture. The horse is the color of a corpse on a battlefield, its rider is Death, and it is followed by a grim companion named Hell (Hades).

The Death riding this pale horse is not the natural death that comes peaceably in old age, but the horrible and destructive death that comes from conquest and war and famine. But that isn't all. John writes that following Death was the grim companion—Hell. In apocalyptic literature the wicked are punished.

John saw the cycle of conquest, war, famine, and death in the first century. He saw that while Rome struggled for life, it would end in Death. Even as the evil power structures fought to win, defeat would come. And this cycle is repeated in every century. One million Russians died during the nine-hundred-day siege of Leningrad by the German army in World War II. Six million Jews perished in the concentration camps of Europe between 1940 and 1945. And the ongoing struggle of American GIs who returned from Vietnam are vivid reminders of the horror of war. More recently, in Sudan, hundreds of thousands of people have died, and millions been displaced, in genocide perpetrated against several ethnic groups by the Sudanese government and its military. The horror of war in the nineteenth, twentieth, and twenty-first centuries is as ghastly and obscene as it was in the first century.

And so we ask, "How does Christ relate to such grim realities of history and current events?" The answer comes through this striking scene as John tells his first-century readers, and us, that Rome's power, or any military power, is a futile cycle of conquest, war, revolt, famine, and death. It is true that those who are disobedient and turn their backs on God have a high price to pay for refusing to live creative and redemptive lives for the Lord, but we know that the real victory of history comes through the saving action of Jesus Christ and the faithfulness of Christians to Him.

The lesson for all time is clear: Anyone who tries to save his or her life at the expense of others will self-destruct. It is only by giving our lives in service that we achieve our true personhood. Jesus put it this way: "Whoever finds their life will lose it, and whoever loses their life for my sake will find it" (Matthew 10:39, NIV). To hate another person, to connive to get even or ahead of someone else, to maliciously put another person down, is death to the soul.

But while the four horsemen thunder across the stage of history, it is the Lamb, Christ, who controls the seals. It is He who is in charge; Christ presides over history. Revelation is a book of hope. John's message here must have given enormous encouragement to those beleaguered Christians in the seven churches in a Rome-dominated world ruled by a sadistic madman.

That same word of hope can make a difference today in spite of the modern horrors that threaten the peace of our world. We worry about new and unknown viruses, we worry that new technologies such as artificial intelligence will eventually spell doom and massive destruction for humanity. Enormous energy is spent in hating people who are unlike us. But our hope and our confidence are in Christ, Who could open the seals in Revelation and Who knows the book of history.

But there is more. As people living in an enormously complex world, turmoil so often rages in our inner being. The four horsemen can so easily ride roughshod over our emotions—"war" can rage deep down inside of us. Self-doubt, insecurity, feelings of defeat and unworthiness drive us into depression. So often we feel alone and deserted, convinced that nobody really cares. But there's a personal message in this part of our lesson that assures us that Christ is in charge of our circumstances. He can turn our defeats into victory.

Stop a moment now and read the apostle Paul's great declaration of victory in Romans 8. Here he insists that in all "things we are more than conquerors through him that loved us." And then he goes on to say, "For I am persuaded, that neither death, nor life, nor angels, nor principalities, nor powers, nor things present, nor things to come, nor height, nor depth, nor any other creature, shall be able to separate us from the love of God, which is in Christ Jesus our Lord" (8:38–39, KJV). That is the grand "Hallelujah" chorus for every Christian in today's world.

## The Suffering of God's Persecuted Witnesses (6:9–11)

When Christ, the Lamb, opened the fifth seal, John saw those who had died for their faith as martyrs, many of them killed by Emperor Domitian's orders. Earlier, John had already mentioned Antipas (2:13). If we had been members of any one of the seven churches in Asia, we could have accepted John's picture of the four horsemen as agents of God's judgment on an evil world, but we would still desperately need the answer to this question: "John, what has happened to my friend Antipas and all the other Christians who were slaughtered by Domitian?"

### *The Place of the Martyrs*
John answers that question in verse 9 with colorful and picturesque language. "I saw under the altar the souls of those who had been slain because of the word of God and the testimony they had maintained" (NIV). It was a popular Jewish

belief that the original model of the Jerusalem temple was in heaven. And so what we have here in this verse is a picture that is obscure to us but familiar to John's first readers.

Jewish ritual in the tabernacle and the temple provided for the sacrifice for sin to be made on the fourteen-foot-high altar. However, some of the blood from the animal sacrifice was to be applied to the four horns of the altar, and the rest was to be poured "at the base of the altar of burnt offering at the entrance to the tent of meeting" (Leviticus 4:7, NIV).

The picture here then is that the blood of those who had been martyred for their faith, including Antipas, was "under the altar." In other words, their blood had been shed—they had been killed—as an offering to God. Yes, by their refusal to worship Domitian and call him "lord," they had signed their own death warrant. Yet the reward for their faithfulness was indeed a place in heaven with the Lord.

### An Appeal for Vengeance?

Next John tells us that he heard those martyrs cry with "a loud voice, saying, 'How long, O Lord, holy and true, will You refrain from judging and avenging our blood on those who dwell on the earth?'" (6:10, NASB). This is a hard question! But how often have we asked "why"? When we have been persecuted—criticized and condemned—how often have we wished that God would lash out at those who have wronged us? Why doesn't God clobber them?

But in God's plan there was and is a better way, and we have it in verse 11. First, while those martyrs might have been seen as losers by their pagan neighbors, from God's perspective they were winners. They were given white robes, symbols of victory and purity. Second, they were told to "rest for a little while longer" (6:11, NASB). God can be depended upon to act in His good time. Third, other fellow Christians were yet to qualify for the victor's crown. Evil will be overcome by the faithfulness of Christians who are willing to literally lay their lives on the line for Christ.

Again, there is an application here for our time. We are part of an "instant" culture. We want things to happen now, within the brackets of our understanding of time. But both the Psalmist and the prophet Isaiah have important words of counsel for us: "Wait on the Lord: be of good courage, and he shall strengthen thine heart: wait, I say, on the Lord" (Psalm 27:14, KJV). And, "But those who wait for the Lord [who expect, look for, and hope in Him] will gain new strength and renew their power; they will lift up their wings [and rise up close to God] like eagles [rising toward the sun]; they will run and not become weary, they will walk and not grow tired" (Isaiah 40:31, AMP). It was this kind of encouragement and assurance that Christians of all time so urgently need.

## The Outcome of Evil—the Universe in Upheaval (6:12-17)

The opening of the sixth seal brought on a cataclysmic upheaval: the entire physical universe began to rip apart at the seams. The toll of sin is devastating and awesome. And so the apocalyptic writings of that time pictured the end of time as being ushered in by terrible events. The imagery is rich in the Old Testament setting and in the apocalyptic writings that appeared after Malachi and into the first century AD.

John writes of seeing a universal upheaval—a gigantic earthquake shook the earth, moving mountains and islands out of their places; the sun was dark and the moon turned red so it didn't give off light; the stars and planets were shaken loose from their orbits; there was an awesome upheaval in the heavens. All these signs and happenings are referred to in the Old Testament and apocalyptic writings, and all were familiar to John's first readers.

So terrible was the picture John saw that all humankind— "kings of the earth, the princes, the generals, the rich, the mighty, and everyone else, both slave and free" (NIV)—tried to escape and hide, as most English Bible versions translate it, "from the wrath of the Lamb" (6:15–16).

Our picture here is a vivid one of God's judgment on evil and evil people at the end of time as we know it. The horror of sin is that it means separation from God, both now and in the future. Evil may seem to win out for a time, but first-century and twenty-first-century Christians alike need to know that God's Word is always the last word.

## The Church Defeated but Victorious (7:1–17)

We've seen in our lesson as we've studied the six seals that evil, symbolized by the four dread horsemen, will ride across history from the first coming of Christ until His Second Coming. But violence of this kind is deceptive and always self-destructive. To the first-century world, Rome looked victorious as the ruler of the world. But in reality, the seeds of defeat had been sown, and it was only a matter of time before the empire would crumble.

Now, in this part of our Scripture lesson the depth of focus increases. We draw nearer to the throne of God and see that the church is guaranteed safety even as the unbelieving world reels toward self-destruction. We see, too, that while Christians may have to endure hard times and even suffering, their eternal safety is assured. The four horsemen cannot defeat or destroy the church. This was precisely the encouragement those Christians needed in the Asian churches. At the same time, we gain confidence and encouragement in being reminded through this study that nothing, *absolutely nothing*, can defeat us in our Christian pilgrimage as our faith is firmly fixed in Jesus Christ.

### Sealing God's Servants—the 144,000

John begins this vision, which is rich in picture language, by letting us see that God has put a restraint on evil (7:1–8). We've already seen that He can bridle the four horsemen. Now we have a picture of four angels at the four "corners" of the world ready to unleash crosswinds that will produce destructive results.

There was the feeling among people during the early periods of time that when winds originated directly from the north, south, east, or west, they would be friendly and favorable. But crosswinds that blew diagonally would be destructive. The picture here is of four angels positioned at each "corner" of the earth getting ready to unleash crosswinds that will be destructive. And especially destructive was the wind from the southeast that rolled in from the deserts with blast-furnace intensity.

But we are told that destructive winds are being restrained until an angel can fix a seal on the foreheads of God's people (7:4). Just as the ancient Israelites escaped the angel of death in Egypt by having blood sprinkled on their doorposts (Exodus 11–12), so the people of God will be spared by having God's seal on their foreheads.

A seal in ancient times was a sign of ownership. Kings throughout history wore signet rings that were used to make an impression on sealing wax, which in turn indicated that a document or an item was authentic. The seal was a sign of ownership. And so we have the angel from the east with "the seal of the living God" (Revelation 7:2, most translations) ready to put His stamp of ownership on His people.

We also discover in verse 4 that John heard in his vision that 144,000 people received the ownership seal of the living God. The number 144,000 (12 × 12 × 1000) is a whole number indicating completeness. This number represents all true believers. It implies there are no limitations, and it refers to the Old Testament faithful and the New Testament Christians of all time.

In other words, as servants of God and believers in Jesus Christ, *we are sealed and secure*. We are among the 144,000 because we are sealed by the Spirit of God. Even though we are Gentiles, as a part of the church—the new Israel, according to the New Testament—we are the inheritors of the titles and privileges of the old Israel. And so, with the 144,000, we have another of the symbolic figures of Revelation that represents the totality and completeness of God's faithful people.

### The Multitude in White Robes

Now, in John's vision the 144,000 were people on earth. But the scene changes as John shifts our attention to heaven and speaks of "a great multitude that no one could count, from every nation, tribe, people and language, standing before the throne and before the Lamb. They were wearing white robes and were holding palm branches in their hands" (7:9, NIV).

What is the relationship between the earthly group of 144,000 and the multitude that make up the heavenly group? They are one and the same. John has given us two visions, or one vision in two parts, to drive home the point once and for all that the people of God are safe and victorious.

In powerful picture language we are made to see that the countless multitude of God's people in all time is—universal. In this scene we catch the glorious inclusiveness of the Good News as we see this vast throng clustered close to God and to Christ holding palm branches of victory in their hands.

Next John heard what must have been one of the most stirring sounds to strike anyone's ears as this vast heavenly crowd shouted, "Salvation belongs to our God who sits on the throne, and to the Lamb" (7:10, NASB). And then came the grand crescendo as all the angels and elders and other inhabitants of heaven joined in one awesome act of worship, "Amen, blessing, glory, wisdom, thanksgiving, honor, power, and might belong to our God forever and ever. Amen" (7:12, NASB).

The magnificent scene described is thrilling and encouraging in the truest sense of the word. There are times when we are inclined to be discouraged. There are some days it seems that for every step forward we take we stumble back two steps. At such moments we take our eyes off the Lord and turn them to circumstances and people. But the great news from these scenes in John's visions is that as believers in Jesus Christ, the Lamb, God's seal is on us. We are a part of His family, and we can shout with God's children of all time, "Salvation belongs to our God."

### The Lamb Who Is the Shepherd

Next, in this closing part of our lesson, an elder, to be sure that John has properly identified the heavenly multitude, not only explains who they are and where they came from, but he also tells him about their future (7:13–17).

The elder makes it clear that the throngs John sees clustered around God's throne are the ones that came out of the great tribulation. This is not a general reference to tribulation but to a specific time of terrible distress foretold by Jesus in Matthew 24:21 and Mark 13:19. The word here is that Christ had seen all of these people through that time of suffering. At the same time, though, John's first readers would have taken comfort in our Lord's faithfulness to them in their time of persecution and tribulation, even as we are challenged by this assurance in our time.

The elder makes it clear that these who came out of the great tribulation had their robes washed and made "white in the blood of the Lamb" (7:14, most translations). Again, we're confronted by a colorful metaphor. For us, flowing blood reminds us of death. We speak of getting sick at the sight of blood. But for John's Jewish readers blood spoke of life. The "blood of the Lamb"—of Christ—is representative of everything He did so we might have life. We are saved by His blood!

Finally in verses 16 and 17 our attention is shifted from the present to the future, and we are shown the ultimate destiny of the people of God. What marvelous words John gives us here: "'Never again will they hunger; never again will they thirst. The sun will not beat down on them,' nor any scorching heat. For the Lamb at the center of the throne will be their shepherd; 'he will lead them to springs of living water.' 'And God will wipe away every tear from their eyes'" (NIV).

What a tender and assuring picture of the future! John has given us here a lovely assurance that God's faithfulness stretches beyond our lives here on earth.

Still, we might be tempted to ask, "What's the value of talking about the by-and-by?"

The resounding answer is "Because it helps us in the here-and-now." We desperately need the assurance that the same Lord who is with us day after day now will also be with us when we move out of the present into the unknown of the future.

The closing words of our scripture lesson remind us of the classic image of the shepherd caring for his sheep. In the Psalms we are told that the "LORD is my shepherd" (23:1, KJV); John writes in his Gospel that Jesus says, "I am the good shepherd" (John 10:11, ESV). The writer of the letter to the Hebrews speaks of Jesus as "the great Shepherd of the sheep " (Hebrews 13:20, NASB).

With such a Lamb, with such a Shepherd, with such a Christ—we can move boldly into each new day without any fear for the future. He is in charge!

*Lord God, I am so grateful for Your faithfulness, Your never-failing presence. To know that Your covenant love extends beyond this life comforts and consoles me.* AMEN.

# PHILADELPHIA

Like the other six churches who were the recipients of the letter describing John's visions, Philadelphia was located in what is now Turkey. It was located some twenty-six miles south and east of Sardis on an important Roman road that connected the west part of the Roman Empire with the east. In AD 17 the city was leveled by a shattering earthquake; however, it was quickly rebuilt and renamed twice in the first century. Virtually nothing remains of the city John knew. It is situated in a modern municipality and district called Alaşehi. Today the area is known for its production of sultana raisins and other fruit. In Revelation, Philadelphia and Smyrna were praised by Jesus for their faithfulness, and some churches today include Philadelphia as part of their church name to indicate their desire to follow in these early Christians' footsteps.

# Notes

# Notes

# The Judgment of the Trumpets—How Evil Punishes Itself

*Dear Lord Jesus, thank You for the hedge You've placed around me—protecting me from all evil, not allowing it to enter my heart or spirit. Help me to remember that You are my shield and the lifter up of my head. AMEN.*

Both we and John's first readers in the seven churches eagerly await the opening of the seventh seal of history because we fully expect it to give us a panoramic view of the End Time. But this doesn't happen. Instead we are to see a vision of seven angels with seven trumpets and are given a "flashback" on the history we have covered with the opening of the first six seals. This time we go back over the same territory but from a different perspective.

What is the difference? When the six seals were broken, we were shown what will happen in history up to the Second Coming of Christ with reference to Christians and the hard times of suffering they are called to endure. And we got the good news that the church, the Body of Christ, will not only survive but will thrive as well.

Now the seven angels with the seven trumpets go back over that same period of history, up to and including the Second Coming of Christ. But this time the focus is on the world of ungodly human society—those who have refused to follow Christ, the Lamb of God.

Here we see that bad people always destroy themselves. Sin is its own worst enemy. The trumpets blare this warning to an unbelieving world—the choice to live in darkness leads to an "outer darkness." At the same time, though, the angels with the trumpets give assurance that God is gracious; He doesn't want Rome or any other nation to destroy itself. There is always the promise that if the prodigal will come back to his senses, the Father will receive him and celebrate his return (Luke 15).

## The Seventh Seal—God Hears His People's Cry (8:1–5)

### A Half Hour of Silence

With the opening of the seventh seal, the mood changes drastically. Up till now there had been shouts of praise and vigorous singing. But now John writes, "When the Lamb opened the seventh seal, there was silence in heaven for about half an hour" (8:1, ESV). Silence—what an ominous change for many of us. Silence is something we have difficulty coping with; we become uneasy.

And yet the Psalmist wrote, "Be still, and know that I am God" (46:10, KJV). The prophet Isaiah worded it this way: "In quietness and in confidence shall be your strength" (Isaiah 30:15, KJV). We're reminded, too, of the story of Elijah in the wilderness of the Negev listening for the voice of God. It wasn't in the strong and rushing wind or in the earthquake or in the fire. But in the silence the Lord spoke to the prophet in "a still small voice" (1 Kings 19:11–12, KJV).

Most of us are very often so busy broadcasting that we have no time or "ear" to receive. And yet frequently God uses the silence to speak to us as He did with the boy Samuel (1 Samuel 3).

### The Seven Angels

But now in our lesson John seems to use this half hour of silence as a suspense builder before he shows us God's next dramatic history lesson. And that begins to unfold as he next writes, "And I saw the seven angels who stand before God" (8:2, NIV). Many of John's readers were familiar with these seven angels since they were prominent in the Jewish intertestamental literature of that time (Tobit and Enoch). They were known as the "Angels of the Presence" who stood before God to pass on to Him the prayers of the faithful. One of these is named by the writer of Tobit: "I am Raphael, one of the seven holy angels, which present the prayers of the saints, and which go in and out before the glory of the Holy One" (12:15 Tobit, KJV).

We are told next in verse 2 that each of the seven angels was given a trumpet—the favorite musical instrument of apocalyptic writers. The trumpet directs people's attention to God and symbolizes His movement in history. Here, too, the symbolism is rich in Old Testament history.

We first meet the "voice of the trumpet" in Exodus 19:19 (KJV) as Moses and the children of Israel stood before God at the foot of Mount Sinai where its voice "grew louder and louder"

(ESV). It was then that "Moses spoke, and God answered him in thunder" (19:19, ESV). In all, there are at least twenty-one references to the trumpet in our Old Testament scriptures, the last of which appears in Zechariah 9:14 where the prophet writes, "The Sovereign Lord will sound the trumpet" (NIV).

### Another Angel Moves into the Scene

Now the action in John's vision begins to pick up as he sees another angel approach the altar in heaven. Other parts of the picture include "a golden censer," "much incense," "the smoke of the incense," "fire from the altar," and finally, "peals of thunder, rumblings, flashes of lightning, and an earthquake" (8:3–5, ESV).

### A Golden Altar

Earlier, when the fifth seal was opened, John saw another altar, and he wrote, "I saw under the altar the souls of them that were slain for the word of God" (6:9, KJV). These were the martyrs who had given their lives rather than knuckle under to worship the caesars. But now John saw a golden altar that contained, as it were, the prayers of the people of God. And then he saw the coals of fire from the altar ignite the incense—a symbol of prayer—and, mixed with the prayers of the saints, it "rose before God from the hand of the angel" (8:4, ESV).

### God Hears Their Prayers

This picture language tells us that while nobody had paid any attention to the suffering of the Christians in the seven churches at the hands of Domitian, their prayers for deliverance were not lost. God had not ignored them. God had not forgotten the "How long?" cry of the martyrs, for John in his vision saw that God would act against the evil forces of Rome that had seemed to have the upper hand against the Christians.

The next action of the angel spells destruction and death to the proud, arrogant, and brutal Roman Empire as he "took the censer, filled it with fire from the altar, and hurled it on the earth" (Revelation 8:5, NIV), and then came the thundering and lightning and earthquakes. The "enlightened" people of Rome had never dreamed that their future was tied to the prayers of the Christians they tried to get rid of.

## God Hears Our Prayers

The symbolic action described here in this colorful scene is a reminder to us that God has heard the prayers of His people in every century, and He hears ours today. In our humanness and limited sense of time, we may not see some of the answers God has for us, but in a way that we are unable to comprehend, we have the assurance that we've been heard. We understand the scene we've just viewed through John's eyes as a prelude to the blowing of the seven trumpets, which is a warning of judgment and a call to repentance.

## The Coming Death of Rome

The decline and fall of the Roman Empire is antiquity's most terrible and instructive lesson. This remarkable city-state, piling success upon monumental success, seemed indestructible. And then, having conquered the known world, it enmeshed itself and civilization in catastrophe. Edward Gibbon, the illustrious historian, gave us a penetrating and sustained account of this greatest phenomenon of history, and in a somber moment he said that Rome's story was little more than the register of its crimes, follies, and misfortunes.

Gibbon detected and evaluated a number of reasons for the destruction and death of that great empire. Among them he lists these three: natural calamities, inner rot and decay, and the invasion of the barbarians.

The first four trumpets in our Revelation lesson sound the note of the natural calamities that struck Rome (8:7–13). The fifth trumpet sounds the note of inner rot and decay. Trumpet six depicts the invasion of a demonic army of two hundred million from the east—the barbarian invasion. Gibbon's *Decline and Fall of the Roman Empire* is widely seen as one of the most accurate and significant histories of ancient Rome ever written. But John, through his vision, anticipated Gibbon's judgments by many centuries. No, Rome's funeral didn't catch God by surprise.

## Nature Warns an Unbelieving World (8:6–13)

This next part of John's vision shows us that God the Creator can use nature to combat the sins of Rome and come to the support of the persecuted Christians. History reveals that whenever sin and evil go unchecked, even the natural order of things may be used by God in judgment.

### The First Trumpet

The first trumpet (8:7) brought a shower of "hail and fire, mixed with blood" (ESV) that destroyed a third of the earth's greenery. This impressionistic scene is John's way of saying symbolically that even earth's greenery recoils in horror at Rome's evil society. The hail, fire, and blood symbolize any kind of evil and destructive forces that are unleashed at any time on our earth.

The plagues that struck at Egypt at the time of the Exodus (Exodus 9:24) give us the background imagery for these disasters. The various plagues that assailed the Nile Valley in those days were God's way of getting Pharaoh to repent, to change his mind and release the Israelites.

It is interesting and important to notice that each of these "trumpet plagues" affects only one-third of the earth. This is because in the book of Revelation fractions represent incompleteness. Through this we see just how patient and long-suffering God is. In exacting only partial judgment, God has given humanity time to repent of its sin.

We have reminders even today of how nature responds to human selfishness and greed. In this first catastrophe the green grass symbolizes the earth's very life. And even this can wither and burn because of Rome's sins.

### The Second Trumpet

First, a third of the earth is devastated and its greenery destroyed (8:7). Now, with the sound of the second trumpet, catastrophe strikes at the sea as a flaming mass resembling a mountain falls into it (8:8–9). As those early Christians read this vivid account of disaster, they may well have been reminded of the legend of Atlantis. And it is possible that they related this cataclysmic event with the eruption of

Mount Vesuvius, which destroyed the cities of Herculaneum and Pompeii and wrought havoc on the Bay of Naples. Then, too, they had probably read in the apocryphal *Sibylline Book V* about how a flaming star fell into the sea and burned it up.

But a picture of devastation that affected the ocean was certainly not limited to the first century. Through our thoughtlessness and carelessness we are contributing to the violation of our oceans with oil spills that pollute and blacken beaches. Ocean beds are becoming dumps for nuclear waste, beaches are strewn with mountains of detritus and debris, and the senseless slaughter of whales and other sea life is wiping out entire species of God's creatures that have inhabited the oceans since the beginning of time. Yes, the destruction of the oceans takes many forms, including the calculated action of insensitive people.

## The Third Trumpet

The trumpet message of the third angel brought about the pollution of the freshwater streams and rivers as a star called Wormwood plunged down from heaven and made the water bitter. While we can't explain the star symbol in this scene, we do have an explanation for the Wormwood symbol. Wormwood is a plant that is bitter to the taste, and it symbolized the bitterness of God's judgment on sinful people.

Our picture here is of an evil that is too bitter to live with. And yet not all is lost, for, as with the other scenes, the devastation struck only a third of the streams. There was even yet the opportunity to repent and avoid total destruction.

### The Fourth Trumpet

With the blast of the fourth trumpet (8:12) the heavenly bodies—sun, moon, and stars—lost one-third of their brightness so that both night and day lacked the usual amount of light.

To speculate on how this could happen is futile and misses the point. The idea that John wants to communicate here is that the lights are going out all over the world. Rome has already fallen into one-third darkness. But the trumpet sound serves as a warning. It isn't too late. What light exists is only possible because God is restraining His judgment.

### An Important Pause

In this pause (8:13) we have an eerie picture of an eagle flying through the heavens shouting, "Woe! Woe! Woe . . . !" (NIV). Other versions translate "woe" as "alas," "terror," or "trouble." The warning is clear. No power structure or person can get away with evil. By killing Christians, Rome was devising her own doom. Payday will come eventually. We will reap what we have chosen to sow.

The cry of alarm sounded here is a reminder to us that we choose our future. The choices we make today will affect what we are tomorrow.

The cry of alarm is also a warning that if we fail to repent and change our ways after the first four trumpet-plagues, things will get worse. The one-third will become two-thirds, and eventually three-thirds. Rome was to see that she had suffered indirectly as the first four trumpets affected the environment. But she would come to see that the remaining three trumpets had a message that would affect her more directly.

# The Torment of Inner Moral Decay (9:1–12)

## *The Fifth Trumpet*

Now the portrayal of terror takes on a sinister note. It is no longer nature but demonic beings that are on the attack. At the trumpet blast John "saw a star fallen from heaven to earth, and he was given the key to the shaft of the bottomless pit" (9:1, ESV). People in the first century saw a close link between stars and angels, so it would seem that John is referring here to an evil angel, one that had the "key to . . . the bottomless pit."

Many ancient Romans believed that evil angels and other demonic forces and beings were held prisoner in an underworld from which they could not escape except through volcanic eruptions. They further believed that the exit from below into the volcanic cone that led to the surface was protected by a door that was kept locked. This might well have been the picture John had in mind as he wrote these words.

This bottomless pit or abyss held a vast reservoir of evil. As John watches, smoke pours up through the shaft and fills the air. Through the smoke he sees an enormous swarm of locusts emerging. But these aren't ordinary locusts. John tells us their sting was like that of scorpions, and then he goes on in these verses to describe the rest of their appearance and actions in a way that sounds like a modern horror movie. The description in verses 4–10 is enough to strike terror into the hearts and minds of even the bravest as these creatures are pictured attacking people.

We might well ask, "What is the significance of this horror picture?" The most likely answer is that John intends for us to see the inner moral sickness of the Roman Empire. The locust was a symbol of destruction, and Rome was being eaten from within by destructive forces that produced inner rot and decay.

Moral depravity ate away at the foundation of the once great Roman society, much like termites and locusts slowly but thoroughly devastate a wood structure or a grain-laden field. In the same way, dishonesty, corruption, and moral decay will destroy any culture or nation, no matter how privileged it is. Evil forces are operating in the world in every century. Domitian saw himself as the god Apollo, an incarnate deity, and his maniacal shoes have been filled in our time by Stalin, Hitler, Amin, Mao, Pinochet, and Kim Jong Un.

But the good news is that Christians are assured of being victorious over this moral darkness (John 1:5). And the word given to us here in this part of our scripture lesson is that the demonic forces loose in the world are not as powerful as they seem. They can kill and they can torment for only a short period of time (9:5). Though we should be cautious about underestimating the devil, we must also take care to not over-rate him.

As horrible and graphic as this picture of terror and evil is, we, as Christians, need to remember that to be overly pre-occupied with the power of the demonic is in itself demonic. Instead, our energies are to be concentrated on the power of God. As sons and daughters of God, we are to be "salt" and "light" in an unbelieving world. The Lord has given us the power to offset the destructive forces of decay.

# Barbaric Evil Is Destroyed by the Barbarians (9:13–21)

## The Sixth Trumpet

The sixth trumpet sounds Rome's last warning. When the seventh trumpet blows, it will already be too late. The warning this time is death—one-third of all humankind is doomed to die. But again, we're dealing with the fraction, and there is still time for Rome to repent of its evil ways. God's patience seems to know no bounds.

We see now in this closing scene of chapter 9 the invasion from beyond the Euphrates of two hundred million—a countless number—of fire-breathing, snake-tailed horses mounted by colorful barbarian riders. This vast cavalry of death rampaged out of Mesopotamia and hit the Roman Empire like a firestorm.

John's first-century readers would have instantly understood his Euphrates-cavalry image. Beyond the Euphrates to the east (modern-day Iran and Turkmenistan) was the great Parthian nation that the Romans had never been able to conquer. The Romans feared the Parthians' crack cavalry in the same way that much of the world fears the terrorist-supporting regimes gaining access to nuclear weapons.

These first-century Parthian horsemen were such skilled archers that they could send an arrow into a Roman soldier while galloping full speed toward him and drive another shaft into him while riding away. This maneuver was referred to as the "Parthian shot."

Rome had disregarded all human decency in its treatment of the Christians. The day was coming when it would be repaid for its reign of terror. And as history now tells us, the empire did indeed fall before a barbarian horde.

While there are details of this vision that are not clear to us, its warning and meaning are unmistakable. Sin and evil never go unpunished. To not repent of evil and violence is to court ultimate disaster.

There's a stark reminder in this scene for us. Barbarism swept through the twentieth century with two global wars and countless smaller wars and "police actions." In the twenty-first century, we live constantly under the threat of a disastrous third world war that will be fought with nuclear weapons as well as chemical and cyber warfare. We possess the technology to incapacitate and wipe out entire civilizations. But the Good News is still with us. It is in Christ, the Prince of Peace, that even in our world we can find peace.

## The Bittersweet Gospel (10:1–11)

### A Mighty Angel Appears

We have a bit of a pause in the action of the angels and the trumpets as John in his vision focuses now on another scene. He writes, "I saw another strong angel coming down from heaven, clothed with a cloud; and the rainbow was on his head, and his face was like the sun, and his feet like pillars of fire" (10:1, NASB). This is certainly no ordinary angel, for we understand here that he came directly from God's presence. He is described as being dressed in a cloud. This image is doubtless drawn from the Psalmist who first wrote, "Bless the LORD, O my soul! O LORD my God, you

are very great! . . . He . . . makes the clouds his chariot"
(Psalm 104:1, 3, ESV).

## A Description of the Mighty Angel

The next word is that this mighty angel has a "a rainbow above
his head" (10:1, NIV). This descriptive image is apparently
drawn from the writings of the prophet Ezekiel in which the
rainbow is described as being part of God's brightness and glory
(Ezekiel 1:28). And the reference to the angel's face looking
like the sun is certainly reminiscent of the description of
Jesus, whose "face shone like the sun" (Matthew 17:2, NASB)
when He was transfigured before His disciples on the mountain.

In verse 2 the mighty angel is described as having "set his
right foot on the sea, and his left foot on the land" (ESV). This
means that his power extended over the entire universe. And
in verse 3 "he gave a loud shout like the roar of a lion" (NIV).
The lion's roar is frequently used to describe the voice of God:
"They shall go after the LORD; he will roar like a lion" (Hosea
11:10, ESV) and "the lion has roared; who will not fear? The
LORD God has spoken . . ." (Amos 3:8, ESV).

## A Study in Contrasts

What an incredibly awesome figure this angel must have been!
The beauty and magnificence of this colorful description must
have lifted the hearts of those hard-pressed Christians in the
seven churches for whom the task of just making it through
each twenty-four-hour day took enormous physical and
emotional energy. There wasn't much beauty in their days.
Life was pretty sordid and cruel. But now John is telling them

about this special angel from God whose very appearance offers reassurance for today and hope for the future.

It is easy for us to identify with those first-century Christians even though most of us are not confronted with the physical abuse that was routine in their lives. We, too, become intensely absorbed in the daily business of living. Intense competition in our business and professional life . . . pressures of inflation, of high interest rates, or, on the other hand, of low interest rates . . . the agonizing uncertainties that are so much a part of earning enough to pay the monthly bills . . . the stomach-churning anxieties that assault us at times in our marriage, home, and family relationships . . . concern for the future—all of these and more press in upon us and rob us of our ability to see God in our world.

But this scene reminds us that there are magnificent "angels" in the nitty-gritty of our days. If we will raise our eyes from the pressures of the ordinary, we can see and feel the beauty and presence of the Creator-God at work in our lives and in the world.

If you've ever been stopped in your tracks by the sight of a dazzling autumn sunset, seen the stars falling from the sky in a meteor shower, or stopped whatever you were doing to share the rare sight of a double rainbow with a loved one, it is easy to see a glimpse of glory. And yet those glorious natural phenomena are but a faint reflection of what John saw and felt as he watched that mighty angel.

### The Scroll and the "Seven Thunders"

In verse 2 John tells us something more about this "mighty" (NIV and other translations) angel: "He was holding a little scroll, which lay open in his hand" (NIV). And as he held that open scroll John says that the "seven thunders" spoke. This expression reminds us of John's words in his Gospel when the people around Jesus who "heard it were saying that it had thundered; others were saying, 'An angel has spoken to Him!'" (John 12:28–29, NASB). But even more descriptive is the seven-part voice of God found in Psalm 29.

Up to this point, John had been writing down everything he saw, but here he says, "I heard a voice from heaven say, "'Seal up what the seven thunders have said and do not write it down'" (10:4, NIV). John was forbidden to write down the message of the "seven thunders," but whatever the message was, the angel who spoke next (10:5–7) seems to be saying that through the six trumpet messages given so far, Rome has received warnings with opportunities to change her ways. But time was drawing to a close, and "there would be no more delay" (10:6, ESV)—doom will be sealed with the sound of the seventh trumpet.

The final scene in chapter 10, verses 8–11, gives us another rather unusual picture. The angel tells John to go to the angel who is holding the scroll and take it from him and eat it. So he writes, "And I went to the angel, telling him to give me the little scroll. And he said to me, 'Take it and eat it; it will make your stomach bitter, but in your mouth it will be sweet as honey'" (10:9, NASB).

These strange words draw their sense from the Psalmist who wrote, "How sweet are [God's] words to my taste, sweeter than honey to my mouth!" (Psalm 119:103, NIV). The little scroll was the gospel message, the Word of God.

And what we see here is that for the hearer of the Word of God who accepts it and acts upon it, it will be sweet to the taste. It will bring joy and victory. But for those who hear the Word and reject it by failing to accept it as the power-force in their lives, it will be bitter as defeat and judgment become their reward.

Separation from God is a bitter and painful experience. It was for the arrogant Romans in the first century, and the alleys of history ever since have been littered by both the "down-and-outers" and the "up-and-inners" who have refused to reach out and "take and eat" the Good News of salvation through Jesus Christ.

In the scene just described in our scripture lesson, to eat the scroll meant to take the Word of God completely into our lives. It is to be a part of us; it is to be the force that energizes everything we do.

## The World Is Warned (11:1–14)

The imagery in chapter 11 of our lesson is some of the most difficult to interpret in the entire book. In fact, it is impossible to be very precise with some of it. Yet there is profound truth contained in these verses that is important to all the rest of our study.

Most of what is said here applies to the world, but in the first two verses John does tell his readers in the seven churches and his readers through all time that the Christian's safety is guaranteed in spite of the outward condition that plagues the world. We are assured here that irrespective of world conditions, "the Lamb" has the last word. There are no boundaries around the Lordship of Jesus Christ.

### The Measuring Rod

First, John speaks of being given a measuring rod or reed. Actually, the rod was a unit of Jewish measure totaling roughly nine feet in length. The idea of measuring was quite prevalent in the writing of the prophets, the likely source of this imagery. However, the measuring image was used not only to determine size but also in terms of preservation.

In these verses John is told to measure the temple, but he is specifically instructed to measure only the inner courts that were reserved for the Jews and the priests. Now, when John wrote these words, the temple had been destroyed by the Roman siege years before in AD 70. This means his readers understood that this was to be interpreted in an allegorical way. And since the church was recognized as the "new Israel," the inner sanctuary referred to the church, the Body of Christ. Everything outside that inner area represented the world.

In symbolic language, John's act of "measuring" meant that under any and all circumstances the Christians would be protected and preserved. But all of the rest of the world—the nonbelievers—would be subject to God's judgment because of their unbelief and rejection of Christ.

### The Two Witnesses

Reference is next made to two witnesses who will preach the gospel for a period of 1,260 days. These two witnesses are pictured as "two olive trees" and "two candlesticks." Both of these images are referred to in Scripture as representing the Christian church, the Body of Christ.

The two witnesses have been variously identified, but the common interpretation is that they are Elijah and Moses— the prophet and the lawgiver who also appeared with Jesus on the Mount of Transfiguration. These two, representing the Law and the Prophets, symbolize the Word of God as it is preached by the people of God in a hostile world of terror.

In verses 7–10 we have a graphic picture of what seems to be the triumph of evil over the two witnesses and the church. But then in verse 11 life is restored and the witnesses ascend "to heaven in a cloud" (11:12, ESV). Multiple translations share this wording.

As would be expected, there has been a great deal of speculation centered on this scene. But the important thing for the purpose of our study is to see in this that God promises His people in every century, irrespective of how many more there are ahead, that He will protect and preserve the church. There is no force that can defeat us.

## The Earthquake

John closes this scene by speaking of a rending earthquake that shook the city as soon as the witnesses had left (11:13). There was extensive damage, but the destruction wasn't total, and John says those who survived "glorified the God of heaven [as they recognized His awesome power]" (AMP). In God's patience there was apparently still time for unbelievers to repent of their sin.

# Destruction of the Destroyers (11:15–19)

## *The Seventh Trumpet*

The scene shifts as John now writes, "The kingdom of the world has become the kingdom of our Lord and of His Christ; and He will reign forever and ever" (11:15, NASB). This is without question a high point in the entire book of Revelation. The words are familiar to us through the magnificent production of Handel's *Messiah*. And the second stanza of the great hymn of worship is now given to us by the "twenty-four elders, who sit on their thrones before God " (11:16, NASB).

God's kingdom now and in the future refers to the time and place of His sovereign rule—where He is in charge. This rule, unlike that of Nero and Domitian, is characterized by mercy and love. But there's more: God's rule is one of justice and truth, life and hope, in a new, golden age of peace. And while this new age hasn't arrived yet, the elders sing with great certainty.

Jesus's defeat of Satan and the powers of darkness was determined on His crucifixion day; now in God's timing the victory is secured. The heavenly choruses in this scene are celebrating God's victory!

## *The Time of Judgment*

Now in verse 18 comes God's great act of judgment on those who have remained unrepentant. The lost are now lost forever because they have been completely influenced by evil forces. Their attitudes and actions are illustrated vividly by the Russian novelist Dostoyevsky's story about a mean old woman. It was believed that she had never done a decent thing in her life, and when she died, she went to the place of torment. But as the angels were reviewing the books of heaven, they discovered, much to their surprise, that at one time she had done a good thing.

On a spring day many years before, she had pulled up a raw onion from her garden and given it to a starving beggar. The angels then decided to get an onion like the one she had given away and dangle it over the pit of torment. She reached up and grasped it, and the angels began to gently lift her out.

As she was being slowly lifted up, the people around her in the pit of torment grabbed her around her waist and legs and hung on for dear life in an effort to escape with her. But she was furious and shouted, "This is my onion, and I'm the only one who can go out with it." And with that she began to thrash around and kick her companions loose. All of her violent activity caused the onion's stem to break, and she fell back into the pit clutching the onion.

It's a simple but compelling story, and the point is clear. Not even God can rescue a person who refuses by attitude and action to repent and change his or her ways.

### The Heavenly Temple

Verse 19 speaks of a heavenly temple in which John sees the "the ark of His covenant" (NASB)—what we know simply as the Ark of the Covenant. Again, the symbolism points to the fact that God never forgets His promises, His covenant.

The Ark symbolized God's presence with His people from the days of the tabernacle in the wilderness until it disappeared in 586 BC. God's covenant and promises to His people Israel remained firm and constant throughout all of Old Testament history. Then with the coming of Christ and the establishment of His new society, the church—the new Israel—we, too, are secure in that covenant.

We twenty-first-century Christians can rely just as strongly on God's promises as our first-century spiritual ancestors in the seven churches of the Roman province of Asia.

*Dear Father, I can trust that You won't forget Your promises— Your covenant of love stands fast. "Great is Your faithfulness! Morning by morning new mercies I see." AMEN.*

# THYATIRA

Approximately forty-four miles south and east of Pergamum (now called Pergamas) was the city of Thyatira (often spelled Thyateira in sources outside the Bible). It is now modern Akhisar in western Turkey, south of Istanbul, about fifty miles from the Aegean Sea. Thyatira is the familiar home of Lydia, the seller of purple goods, who was of such help to the ministry of Paul along with Silas (Acts 16:11–40), and the city itself was known for its fabric-dyeing trade. It was home to numerous guilds in the first century, and references to guilds of dyers have been found in the ruins there. In all probability, this church at Thyatira was a missionary church established there by the Ephesian Christians.

# Notes

# *Notes*

# The Cosmic Battle

*Holy Father, just like these first-century Christians, I'm in a battle—against my unwillingness to submit to You and against the enemy of my soul. Lord, You've already won all my battles. Help me to walk in Your victory.* AMEN.

A t the end of our last lesson, chapter 11 of Revelation, we could naturally think that the story had all been told and all that was left was a "grand amen." We saw the defeat of evil and the triumph of Christ.

But if we had been members of the little church at Philadelphia, for example, we would still be puzzled over this nagging question: "Why are we being subjected to this brutal Roman persecution?"

Now, as we move into this lesson, we finally get an answer: "Satan is the enemy behind it all. He met defeat when Jesus died on Calvary's cross and rose again on Easter morning. And now it seems as if he has turned all of his vicious efforts in our direction. We are a part of the cataclysmic clash between good and evil."

## The Characters in the Conflict (12:1–6)

We come now to John's next vision. And as with each previous vision, this one is rich in imagery and action. The three main characters in this first vision in our lesson are a woman, a child, and a dragon.

## The Woman

This heavenly woman is symbolic of the people of God (12:1). In representing the "old Israel" she produced the Messiah, and in her role as the "new Israel" she is the persecuted church.

At the same time, what we have here is a flashback to the birth of Jesus in Bethlehem, and the pregnant woman is Mary, the mother of the Messiah. Her description is colorful: "a woman clothed with the sun, with the moon under her feet and a crown of twelve stars on her head" (12:1, NIV). In his effort to clothe this woman with divine dignity and beauty, John draws from the Psalms (104) and from the Song of Solomon (6). Jews and Gentiles alike were intrigued by this woman and recognized her nobility.

## The Child

The child, of course, in the vision is symbolic of Jesus Christ, the Messiah. Verse 5 says that this child "is to rule all the nations with a rod of iron" (ESV). This unusual wording takes us back to the second psalm where the reference to the one "with a rod of iron" is most surely a description of the Messiah (Psalm 2:9). And then, of course, following the Messiah's crucifixion and resurrection this "child was caught up unto God, and to his throne" (12:5, KJV).

## The Dragon

The dragon image appears several times in the Old Testament and always as the bitter enemy of God. John's description of this dragon has all of the elements of a horror movie: "a great red dragon having seven heads and ten horns, and on his heads were seven crowns. And his tail swept away a third of the stars of heaven and hurled them to the earth" (12:3–4, NASB).

The seven heads and the ten horns are symbolic of the dragon's tremendous might and power. The seven crowns speak of the dragon's power and authority over the nations of the world. There is more, but this is enough to cast the red dragon as the serpent, the devil, the deceiver, the enemy, and the mighty prince of this world. It was he who tried to kill the child "the moment he was born" (12:4, NIV).

During the time Jesus was on earth Satan made repeated efforts through human agents to destroy Him: Herod's murder of the children in Bethlehem, Jesus's temptations in the wilderness, Judas's betrayal, and the cross.

### The People of God Are Not without Protection

Then upon His return to the Father, when Jesus was out of reach of Satan, the evil one directed his wrath to "the woman." And "the woman fled into the wilderness, where she has a place prepared by God, in which she is to be nourished for 1,260 days" (12:6, ESV).

John could have had any number of sources from which he got this picture. It was not at all uncommon for the early Christians to seek refuge in the deserts and lonely places when they were being maligned and persecuted. And so, as a symbol of the church, the woman finds safety in the lonely places as well as provision for her needs.

In this we also see that although the people of God may have to endure stress for a time, they will be protected and provided for and the period of suffering will end. And this, too, is our promise. Being a Christian isn't necessarily a ticket to a trouble-free life. We'll have our hard times; we'll suffer moments of acute disappointment. Our lives won't be free from pain or the taste of death and the loss of loved ones. But we don't have to handle any of these difficulties alone. God is with us. His promise of victory is ours.

Around the world, Christians have at times, including today, been called upon to endure hardship—and even death—for their faith. Satan is not idle these days in his vengeful pursuit of believers in Christ. But the message of John in our lesson is one of hope and deliverance. God's seal is upon His people.

## The War in Heaven (12:7–17)

In John's vision now we see two mighty forces locked in deadly combat: "And there was war in heaven: Michael and his angels fought against the dragon; and the dragon fought and his angels" (12:7, KJV). Again, these images have a rich background in the Bible. Michael is mentioned as the arch-angel who leads the forces of righteousness against the evil one. We saw him last in Jude 9. There the writer speaks of Michael contending with the devil over the body of Moses.

So now in these eleven verses those Christians in Asia Minor learn why they are under such an evil and furious attack: They are a part of the war that is going on. And this war is still with us. Satan understands God's timing, and in terms of the endless ages of time, he senses his time is getting short.

But John's vision into the future continues, and in verses 8 and 9 we have the word that the forces of Michael and his angels win the war against the dragon: "And the great dragon was thrown down, that ancient serpent, who is called the devil and Satan, the deceiver of the whole world—he was thrown down to the earth, and his angels were thrown down with him" (12:9, ESV).

### The Dragon Is Identified

For John's first readers, the dragon is now identified for the first time. The reference to "that ancient serpent" takes us back to the earliest beginnings of the human race and to Genesis 3. The name *devil* means "slanderer," and Satan means "adversary." In the Old Testament, Satan shows up at times as a sort of cosmic force for evil; a particular case in point is the description in Job 1:6.

Satan lost his battle at Calvary's cross, and now in the vision we see that he could not prevail against the "woman"—the church (12:13). And from there he went to make war "on the rest of her offspring" (12:17, ESV)—the faithful wherever they are. The point is that Satan is at war with the entire human race. But for all who put their faith in Christ, the battle has been won. We just need to claim the victory.

### The Real Enemy of the Seven Churches

And now those Christians in Philadelphia and the other six churches knew who the real enemy was. It was Satan, the age-old enemy of God. Satan was behind their persecution by Emperor Domitian.

## The Enemy's Defeat

But they also had the good word that Satan's defeat was sure. In fact, in the marvelous words of praise found in verses 10–12, those who had died for their faith were lauded as victors over the dragon as John quoted the voice from heaven, "And they overcame him by the blood of the Lamb, and by the word of their testimony; and they loved not their lives unto the death" (12:11, KJV). This is without doubt one of the greatest sentences in all of the Bible.

The Good News for Christians of every century is that Christ through His death and resurrection on the cross conquered the power of Satan, and we, as daughters and sons of God, are privileged to share in that victory. Satan may mobilize his forces against us, but like the woman in the vision, God will rescue us on "the two wings of a great eagle" and keep us from harm (12:14, NIV).

## An Application for Today

On the surface, as we think of the daily routines of our lives, all of this may seem a little far out. We're not threatened with physical persecution and death—most of us. But we are threatened by the subtle attacks of the evil one. Satan can get to us in a variety of ways. We're tempted to misrepresent a product we're selling; we rationalize fudging on our income tax; we steal time from our employer by doing something or going somewhere that is quite apart from our duties. Then, too, Satan sometimes accomplishes his purpose in our lives by using wedges of misunderstanding to damage marriage and family relationships; Christian fellowship becomes impaired in the church because of jealousy over position or sharp differences over what is "Christian" and what isn't.

In other words, Satan has won his point any time he can inspire division, hurt feelings, the determination to get even when we think we've been wronged, and getting us to choose sides and take up "arms" in a church squabble. Then again, sometimes Satan is able to get to us by inspiring in us feelings of self-righteousness and smugness, and we become comfortable and apathetic. We usually classify sin as doing something wrong, but it can also mean not doing anything at all.

We're just as vulnerable to the vicious attacks from the evil one in the twenty-first century as were our spiritual ancestors in the first century. But John's message to us in this part of our lesson is that through the cross and the Resurrection of Jesus we can have victory over anything that threatens to make us less than what God wants us to be.

## Satan's First Beastly Henchman (13:1–10)

The imagery and color in John's vision continues. As we've said so often before, much of this seems unintelligible on the surface, but John's first readers in the seven churches understood the symbolism because they saw in it a picture of their very real struggle.

In chapter 13 of Revelation the curtain is pulled back so that we can see a portrait of two of Satan's violent allies in his battle for supremacy in the first century. First, in this section John "saw a beast rising out of the sea, with ten horns and seven heads, with ten diadems on its horns and blasphemous names on its heads" (13:1, ESV). This beast from the sea symbolized the Roman Empire. Second, in verses 11–18 we are introduced to a second beast who "came up out of the earth" (KJV).

### The Beast from the Sea

As the Jewish Christians read about this first "beast," their thoughts would likely have immediately turned to that vivid description of the four beasts described in Daniel 7, except in this case the characteristics of those four all seem rolled up into one. Let's look more closely now at this grotesque creature.

### The Beast Is Identified

The sea beast was indeed imperial Rome, the personification of Satan's vile, corrupt, and destructive influence. The seven heads of the beast stood for the seven caesars who had ruled Rome from the time of Christ's crucifixion to the time this was written: Tiberius, AD 14–37; Caligula, AD 37–41; Claudius, AD 41–54; Nero, AD 54–68; Vespasian, AD 69–79; Titus, AD 79–81; and Domitian, who began his reign in AD 81 and was assassinated in AD 96.

In verse 3 John writes that one "of the heads of the beast seemed to have had a fatal wound, but the fatal wound had been healed" (NIV). This quite likely refers to the idea that prevailed in John's time that Emperor Nero did not really die in his suicide attempt but had recovered from his sword wound. Those who propagated this myth believed that Nero had traveled east to link up with the barbarian Parthians and would soon return to rule in Rome again. This ghastly idea struck fear into Roman hearts. The thought of that mad monster returning to power conjured all kinds of terrorist visions.

With the mocking cartoon of this beast rising from the sea, we see that power politics is the essence of this caricature as he aspires to the power and omnipotence of God Himself. Indeed, the evil state of the Roman Empire was the earthly counterpart of Satan's kingdom.

Yet we see in these verses that the beast doesn't have everything his own way. While his attitude and activities are vile and incredibly destructive, limits have been placed on his time—forty-two months (13:5)—and the true believers in Christ refuse to knuckle under and worship him. Christians refused to surrender their spiritual integrity for the sake of patriotism.

### A Dramatic Change of Attitude

As we have moved into our study of Revelation, we sense a drastic shift in attitude toward Rome. You will recall when the Pharisees tested Jesus by asking whether it was lawful for them to pay tribute to Caesar that He replied, "Render therefore unto Caesar the things which are Caesar's" (Matthew 22:21, KJV). And time and again Paul sought the protection of Rome, and indicated that citizens should be subject to the state. He told his readers that rulers were not a terror and that Christians should pay tribute to the government (Romans 13).

But now the attitude is entirely different. In our lesson the Roman state is the vile and grotesque beast from the sea. With Nero's reign an era of terror had been launched. The caesars defied the holy God and demanded for themselves the worship due Him. There was a drastic change in the world between the time Paul wrote his letter to the Roman Christians and the time John wrote these words in Revelation 13.

### The Need for Balance between Romans 13 and Revelation 13

Both Romans 13 and Revelation 13 must be taken into account by the Christian with regard to his or her attitude toward the state. For example, many German Christians, reading only Romans 13, did little or nothing to resist Hitler in his mad rush for power just before and during World War II. But other German Christians like Dietrich Bonhoeffer and Helmut Thielicke balanced Romans 13 with Revelation 13 and resisted—in Bonhoeffer's case to his death at age thirty-nine. Evil often comes in the guise of political power, and certainly Hitler demonstrated what evil can accomplish when it controls the state.

As Christians in the twenty-first century, we must live between Romans 13 and Revelation 13. We must be continually alert to being involved intelligently in the world of politics as a means of guarding against our government being taken over by the "beast." It is God's will that our government uphold law and order, but unless we're careful, Satan can twist this into bad law and tyrannical order.

## Resistance of the Right Kind

Of this we can be sure: the beast from the sea has been and always will be active in world affairs, and Christians will always be tested severely when they oppose him. John Bunyan, the author of *Pilgrim's Progress*, was imprisoned for years in Bedford County Jail for his Christian beliefs. One time when governmental authorities promised to release him if he would keep quiet, he responded, "If you release me today, I will preach tomorrow." And then when he was threatened with life in prison, he said, "I will stay in this jail until moss grows from my eyebrows before I will turn my conscience into a slaughterhouse."

As Christians, we are to pray for our country but never to our country or to those who would lead it. Our consciences cannot go up for sale, whether for fame or power or expediency, nor to avoid hard times of persecution. The change in the early Christians' attitude toward Roman rule came with the serious introduction of caesar worship. This was a compromise that couldn't be accepted then, and it can't be accepted now, irrespective of the form it may take in our time.

## No Resigned Fatalism

This part of our scripture lesson closes with a reference to "perseverance and the faith of the saints" (13:10, NASB). There is no reference here to any kind of resigned fatalism. Christians of any generation can never be sure they will escape emotional or physical persecution. We have no assurance that the events of each day will turn up roses, but we have the resources in Jesus Christ to courageously accept the worst that can come and turn it into victory.

Christians are sometimes accused of dragging their feet on issues of social justice. Let it not be so! Perhaps the most well-known and courageous advocate of social justice in the last century was Dr. Martin Luther King Jr., who stood firmly for the right in the face of local and state powers and insisted that "I've been to the mountaintop . . . . And I've seen the promised land." His words and courage will inspire generations to come.

---

## Satan's Second Henchman (13:11–18)

### *The Beast from Out of the Earth*

We are introduced now in verse 11 to a second beast "coming out of the earth. It had two horns like a lamb, but it spoke like a dragon. It exercised all the authority of the first beast on its behalf, and made the earth and its inhabitants worship the first beast, whose fatal wound had been healed" (13:11–12, NIV).

The second beast was apparently an organization or group that was set up in Asia Minor and perhaps throughout the Roman Empire to enforce worship of the emperor. The power of Rome was given religious and cultic significance through caesar worship. The description of the lamb with two horns but the voice of a dragon is a parody of Christ the Lamb. Pictured here is brutal political power that "got religion." Satan gave power to Domitian and then Domitian delegated his authority to the caesar cults. And then throughout the empire there were temples of caesar worship. The political state in its insatiable thirst for power can wear a "halo" in any time. When the multitudes in Germany shouted "Heil Hitler" at the peak of his power, they did so with an unholy fanaticism. Religious zeal attached to godless causes is usually extremely dangerous.

## The Mission of the Second Beast

The primary task of this "land beast" was to get the people to bow down and worship the first beast, the beast from the sea (13:12)—the power of Rome. And to accomplish this he used brutal coercion, deception, and magic to get the people to do what he wanted. Some of the tricks used to achieve the beast's purposes are listed here: "great signs (awe-inspiring acts)" and fire coming down from heaven (13:13, AMP). And in verse 15 the master act of deception is described: He gave "life unto the image of the beast, that the image of the beast should both speak, and cause that as many as would not worship the image of the beast should be killed" (KJV). The reference here is to images of Emperor Domitian that were in the pagan temples. Apparently through ventriloquism these "god images" spoke.

The Christians were supposed to stand in front of these statues and repeat a religious oath of obedience to Domitian as lord god. When they refused to do this, the statue audibly accused them of treason and they would not receive "a mark in their right hand, or in their foreheads" (13:16, KJV). This mark was necessary as a sort of license to work and carry on their livelihood. In other words, without the mark they had no way to earn a living.

This helps us understand a little better the intense pressures on the Christians in the seven churches. To refuse to worship caesar was to be unpatriotic and made it impossible to earn a living.

Most of us in the Western world have no way to apply this particular part of our lesson to our own experiences. From a patriotic point of view, perhaps the closest we come to it is when some people put Christianity and patriotism on the same level: a patriot is a certain kind of Christian, or a Christian is a certain kind of citizen.

And as for the magic bit, there are always those on the fringe who equate spirituality or faith with unusual feats, of making a show, or working some mystical action as proof that God is with them. This is not the pattern laid down for us by Jesus, the disciples, and the early Christians. (See John 4:48; 20:29.)

### The Number of the Beast

Then in verse 18 we're told that this beast had a number: "This calls for wisdom. Let the person who has insight calculate the number of the beast, for it is the number of a man. That number is 666" (13:18, NIV). Since earliest Christian times there has been speculation as to just what this number means.

It is obviously a bad number, but what does it mean? And why did the beast have a number? What is behind all of this?

In the ancient world the ABCs of the alphabet were used in lieu of special symbols for numbers. For example, in Latin X = 10, C = 100, and M = 1,000. We know these as Roman numerals. But we often do the same sort of thing in English by letting A = 1, B = 2, C = 3, etc. The numerical equivalents of the letters can be added to get the number of a person's name. This has long been a popular form of art. The following inscription was found on the wall of a home in Roman Pompeii: "I love a girl whose name is 545." And when a

Roman teenage boy said, "I've got her number," everyone knew that he had an acute case of puppy love.

So from all of this we see that numbers associated with identity were not the least bit unusual. And so now here in our Revelation lesson we find the number 666 attached to this beast. In this case it identifies the second beast, or false religion. While in those days the number 7 stood for basic truth, the number 6 symbolized the enemy or a lie. To be a 6 was code for missing the mark or of a false religion.

Since this second "beast" so persistently and grossly missed the mark, its number was not merely 6 but 666. And if it was necessary to attach a name or a human identity to that, it was likely to be Caesar Nero. For example, a Hebrew spelling of "Caesar Nero" adds up to these numbers: 100 + 60 + 200 and 50 + 200 + 6 + 50 = 666. And based on the myth that had been going around, it was believed that Nero may have returned from the dead in the form of Domitian. The use of these codes was a safeguard against being charged with treason.

Many scholars of the Bible over the centuries have speculated as to the identity of 666. Many different persons have been associated with the number. But it is widely believed that the identity of 666 was Roman Emperor Nero.

## Satan Versus the Lamb (14:1–5)

### The Other Side of the Battle

In our lesson so far we have gotten a dramatic picture of Satan and his two allies who have forced idolatry on the people. Now John's vision continues: "Then I looked, and behold, the Lamb was standing on Mount Zion, and with Him 144,000 who had His name and the name of His Father written on their foreheads" (14:1, NASB). Now we are given a glimpse of the other side—the Lamb and His allies. The contrasts are deliberate and striking: On one side we've already seen the state system with its political power structures and quasi-religious ideologies, which support and sanction the system. Now over against this we see the Lamb of God's redeemed society, the church, armed with the gospel of truth. In reality, every event of history can be seen in light of these two opposing forces.

In verses 3 and 4 reference is made to the 144,000, symbolizing the faithful of all time who had been redeemed and whose lives were pure and holy, "and in their mouth no lie was found, for they are blameless" (14:5, ESV). John says these "are virgins"—pure in life and worship. The Bible regards idolatry as adultery. From this we see that these Christians had not been involved in the caesar cult, and they had stayed away from the fertility temples where "sacred" prostitution was practiced.

The analogy here is obvious. The redeemed children of God are disciplined in their lifestyle. They are spiritually fit.

## Satan's Cohorts Warned (14:6–13)

John's vision continues as he sees another angel who calls humankind everywhere to repent and believe. The Good News of the "everlasting gospel" (14:6, KJV) is that forgiveness is still possible—the door of salvation is still open, and here we have a grand call to worship: "Fear God and give him glory, because the hour of his judgment has come. Worship him who made the heavens, the earth, the sea and the springs of water" (14:7, NIV).

But immediately following this great invitation a second angel appears on the scene and says, "Fallen! Fallen is Babylon the Great" (14:8, NIV). In the book of Revelation, *Babylon* is the code name for Rome. The angel speaks here as if Rome with all of its rottenness and corruption and brutality had already fallen, and for all practical purposes it had; it was only a matter of time.

But then comes a third angel (14:9) who gives a powerful warning to anyone involved in the caesar cult: "And the smoke of their torment goes up forever and ever, and they have no rest, day or night" (14:11, ESV). In other words, those who persist in their rejection of Christ and continue in pagan worship are subject to God's judgment. Here we have a picture of doom as John picks up on wording very close to that used by the prophet Isaiah (34:8–10).

But then the voice speaks again and pays homage to those "'who die in the Lord from now on . . . that they may rest from their labors, for their deeds follow them!'" (14:13, ESV). While times may have been difficult for these Christians, they now reap the benefits of rest.

## Satan's Cohorts Judged (14:14–20)

The vision continues and here John sees Christ as both King and Judge. Judgment is pronounced on Rome, but it will not be pictured until we get to chapter 19. The picture painted at the beginning of this section would have been quite familiar to the Jewish Christians. The picture of the harvest is drawn from Daniel 7:13–14 and Joel 3:13. Take a moment to read those verses. In other words, the harvest of the earth was "ripe"—the time had come for the wicked to be judged for their behavior.

The Christians in the Asian churches were sorely pressed to hold on to their faith in the face of Rome's cutting persecution. But now in verses 19 and 20 the fall of Emperor Domitian, their Satanic persecutor, is vividly described in a wildly exaggerated form. The closing words speak of a river of blood two hundred miles long and about five feet deep.

As we have seen, apocalyptic writers make their point by exaggeration. But the point was clear to those first readers and its truth is very up to date today: Sin and evil have never won a battle in the panorama of history. While evil can appear to succeed for a time, Christ's victory on Calvary and on Easter morning gives us the last word for our struggles every day.

*Heavenly Father, thank You for Your victory over sin.*
*Let the victory I've studied about be evident in my living—*
*my relationships, my thinking, my choices.* AMEN.

# PERGAMUM

Ancient Pergamum (also known as Pergamon or Pergamos) was situated about sixty-five miles due north of Smyrna and located about fifteen miles inland from the Aegean Sea, and northwest of the modern city of the similarly named Bergama, Turkey. In Roman times this was a beautiful city and a center of caesar worship with its Temple of Roma. Pliny the Elder (AD 23/24–AD 79) called the city one of the most important in the province. The ruins of numerous structures from the city's heyday remain around the ancient city, including the Roman baths complex and royal palaces on the upper Acropolis, which are accessible via the Bergama Acropolis Gondola.

# *Notes*

# *Notes*

# The Climax of God's Wrath and the Seven Mysterious Bowls

◆————————————◆

*Father God, I can sense the work of perfection and completion You're doing in my life. Thank You for working to establish me, make me whole, complete, perfect.* AMEN.

Early in our study of this amazing book, John took us behind the scenes and pictured for us his vision of the seven seals (Revelation 6–7). Next we participated in his vision of the seven trumpets (Revelation 8–11). Now in this lesson our focus is once again on the heavenly scene as John pictures for his readers of all time his vision of the seven golden vials or bowls.

John has carefully led us to this great moment of climax— the time when Satan and all his evil forces are completely destroyed. You will remember that with the opening of the seals only one-fourth of everything was devastated. Then the percentages changed with the sounding of the seven trumpets— one-third of everything was laid waste.

But now, as far as Satan and the forces of evil are concerned, the last hour has struck on God's clock. Up until now the opportunity for repentance had apparently remained open, there had still been time. God's incredible patience still prevailed. But as the "seven bowls of God's wrath" are emptied, God's total and final judgment is not felt by one-fourth or by one-third but by all. Satan's doom is a once-and-for-all reality.

## The Song of Victory (15:1-4)

### The Heavenly Scene

John now writes, "I saw in heaven another great and marvelous sign: seven angels with the seven last plagues—last, because with them God's wrath is completed" (15:1, NIV). But for the moment they remain in the background, and center stage is filled with those Christians who have suffered martyrdom under the brutal viciousness of Emperor Nero and the mad persecution of Emperor Domitian.

The martyrs, according to John's vision, are standing by "what appeared to be a sea of glass mingled with fire" (15:2, ESV). The fire speaks of God's judgment that is soon to be released. But the assembled martyrs are now safe and are participating in a victory celebration.

The scene is strange but very much in the style of the apocalyptic writers. There's a mood here that clashes with our twenty-first-century understanding, but the point is clear: These who have suffered and died for their faith are now seen in a victory celebration. All of this reminds us of those words of Jesus that indicate that those who lose their lives for Christ's sake are indeed the ones who find *life* (Matthew 16:25). This is one of the great paradoxes of life— we receive as we give; we're made full as we empty ourselves.

These martyrs who are pictured here clustered by the fiery sea have been delivered by the same power that acted for Moses and the Israelites on the shore of the Red Sea and for Jesus Christ on the hill of Golgotha. God is mighty and powerful and eternal while Nero is dead, and in AD 96, Domitian will join his predecessor by being assassinated.

It is important that we always remember that Satan was doomed from the beginning. In spite of the way things may look at times, God is always in control. Evil may seem to win out for a time, but God is in charge, and we are witnessing in this lesson the final victory over evil and the evil one.

It is completely out of character for a Christian to go around with a gloomy and pessimistic attitude. A "Chicken Little" Christian who looks and acts as if the sky is about to fall is a sad parody. In and through Christ's victory on Calvary, we are winners, and it is safe to assume that God wants us to act like it. Our song of life isn't a dirge but a grand symphony of praise!

### A Song of Victory

And it is praise and thanksgiving that this great crowd of martyrs are offering to God in John's vision. In fact, John writes, "And they sang the song of Moses, the bond-servant of God, and the song of the Lamb, saying, 'Great and marvelous are Your works, Lord God, the Almighty; righteous and true are Your ways, King of the nations! Who will not fear You, Lord, and glorify Your name? For You alone are holy; for ALL THE NATIONS WILL COME AND WORSHIP BEFORE You, for Your righteous acts have been revealed'" (15:3–4, NASB).

This magnificent song of Moses that we find in Exodus 15:1–19 has long been a vital part of Jewish worship. And as these martyred Christians sing in John's vision, the richness of their song has its roots also in Psalm 86:9, Psalm 89, Psalm 98, Psalm 92:5, Hosea 14:9, and Jeremiah 10:7.

Stop your study for a moment and read these victory verses, beginning with Exodus 15:1–19. This is a soul-lifting experience. What would happen if for the next week we began each day by reading these verses of praise! The words in Revelation 15:3–4 are life-changers!

## God's Inescapable Wrath (15:5–16:1)

### The Seven Angels

Immediately following the magnificent hymn of praise and adoration, the action shifts in John's vision. He writes, "After this I looked, and I saw in heaven the temple—that is, the tabernacle of the covenant law—and it was opened. Out of the temple came the seven angels with the seven plagues. They were dressed in clean, shining linen and wore golden sashes around their chests" (15:5–6, NIV).

The place of worship John saw in his vision was not the Jerusalem temple but the original place of worship that God gave His people following the Exodus—the tabernacle. It was commonly referred to as "the Tent of the Testimony (tabernacle)" (Numbers 17:7, AMP).

The tabernacle, as you will recall, was the place of God's presence. And so, in this scene, the seven angels are pictured as coming from the presence of God. Notice the detail in

John's description as he refers to the angels' clothing: pure and white with a golden girdle. Theirs was a heavenly and priestly dress. As God's messengers, they had come from His presence to fulfill His purpose in the next scene.

Then in verse 7 John tells us that he saw one of the four living creatures give each of the seven angels a golden bowl (or vial). You remember that earlier John gave a brief description of these living creatures. The first was like a lion, the second was like a calf, the third had a face like a man, and the fourth was like a flying eagle (Revelation 4:7). These four creatures symbolize the finest and best in God's world of nature.

### A Vision of Glory

John next tells us that with the delivery of the vials to the seven angels an awe-inspiring scene envelops the heavens that speaks of God's glory in terms that would have been readily understandable to his first readers. Smoke was a common symbol of God's glory in the Old Testament scriptures, and so great was this glory that "no one could enter the sanctuary" (15:8, ESV).

In this scene we get a brief glimpse of the holiness and majesty of our God. Yes, He is a God of love, but at the same time He is the divine Creator of the universe. Yes, He is a God of love, but He is also a God of justice. He continues to be patient with us and all of humankind. But as John's vision now unfolds, there comes a day of judgment that leveled Rome because of its mad and vicious sinfulness, and there will come a time when the sinfulness of unrepentant people will also be judged. And so John writes that he "heard a great voice out of the temple saying to the seven angels, Go your ways, and pour out the vials of the wrath of God upon the earth" (16:1, KJV). The moment of judgment had arrived!

## The Seven Bowls of "God's Wrath" (16:2–21)

### *The Natural Disasters of God's Judgment*

The first four judgments unleashed upon the world by each of the four angels were natural disasters affecting the earth, the sea, fresh water, and the sky (16:2–9).

With the release of God's judgment from the first bowl, an unrepentant human race left on earth, "the people who had the mark of the beast" (16:2, NIV), were attacked by horrible sores reminiscent of the plague that struck the Egyptians many centuries before when they refused to obey the word of God and release the Israelites. As the Romans and sinful humans in all time have discovered, sin and disobedience exact a painful toll. Even in our time, we have seen again and again that "those who live by the gun often die by the gun."

When the second and the third angels released God's judgment and wrath, we witness the vile pollution of the sea and of all fresh water everywhere. Again there is a similarity between these acts of judgment and the plague in Egypt when the waters of the Nile were turned "into blood" (Exodus 7:17, 20, NIV).

With the unleashing of these two plagues, John makes a direct reference to the bloodthirsty Romans and their treatment of Christians as he writes, "For they have shed the blood of saints and prophets, and you have given them blood to drink. It is what they deserve!" (16:6, ESV).

Paul made the point this way when he wrote these words to his Galatian friends: "For whatever a person sows, this he will also reap" (Galatians 6:7, NASB). We become what we give ourselves to. Jesus told a story about a rich farmer who became so consumed by all he had that he ultimately lost it all (Luke 12:16–21). While the imagery here seems to point to the time when Rome will be judged for its bloody persecution of the people of God, we see a just God acting in all time against all that is sinful and evil.

When the fourth angel empties his bowl (16:8–9), the earth is scorched by the heat and fire of the sun. With vivid imagery John is describing here how Rome would be ravaged by fire at the time of the city's fall as judgment against the flaming passions that had ruled her way of life for so long.

The judgment of fire unleashed by this fourth angel may well have its counterpart in our time in the development and production of weapons technology. These hold potential for worldwide disaster that is frightening. And while these have not been unleashed yet, we have to ask ourselves this question: "How much has our preoccupation with weapons development and the associated expense pushed people to desperation and starvation because so much of our resources and energies are funneled to destructive causes?"

Before going on, John tells us that in spite of the intensity of this judgment, those who blasphemed the name of God (16:9) refused to repent of their evil ways. These people, like the Egyptian pharaoh in the early chapters of Exodus, had become so hardened in their resistance of God that they were completely unaffected by the judgment.

In these verses John reminds us of the irrational enigma of evil. It just doesn't make sense. Even after the ten plagues, including the death of the firstborn sons, the Egyptian pharaoh irrationally tried to recapture the Israelites before they crossed the Red Sea. This kind of irrationality was seen toward the end of World War II when Germany desperately needed trains to transport troops to the eastern front to stop the Russian advance. Instead, Hitler insisted, in his mad rage, that trains be used to transport Jews to concentration camps.

This same irrationality continues to spread havoc around the world in the twenty-first century.

### Awe-Inspiring Chaos

The fifth angel emptied his bowl "on the throne of the beast, and its kingdom was plunged into darkness" (16:10–11, ESV). Again, we're reminded of the darkness plague that enveloped Egypt at the time of Moses (Exodus 10:21–23). Darkness produces chaos, and the reference points directly to Rome.

When the Romans refused Christ and launched their bloodbath on the Christians, their whole social and political system was thrown into a chaotic darkness as intense as the ninth plague that settled over Egypt (read Exodus 10:21–23).

The intensity of the political darkness and chaos that followed Nero's sadistic reign and suicide carried over into the doubts, fears, suspicions, and hysteria of Emperor Domitian's reign. A darkness hovered over Rome.

Roman society should have been modeled after the Christian church. An acceptance of the Christian witness would have changed the direction of the Roman Empire. But Satan and his evil forces manipulated Emperor Domitian and inspired the caesar cult. The moral darkness was so great, and Roman society was so enslaved by Satan, that they continued to turn their backs on God, "and they did not repent of their deeds" (16:11, NASB).

This judgment has a powerful message for us today. Increasing insensitivity to the whispering of God's Spirit creates a separating wedge between God and us. To let that wedge widen through disobedience to God's will and purposes for our lives creates a darkness, which if allowed to continue will inevitably plunge us into chaos and confusion. When we look at Rome, we twenty-first-century Christians have a model of destruction—a model to be avoided at all costs.

### The Sixth Judgment

Now the sixth angel makes his appearance, and as he empties his "[bowl] of God's wrath" (16:1, NIV), John sees in his vision the dry bed of the Euphrates River. This sight must have reminded him of the several references in the Old Testament scriptures where God had exercised His power by causing water to dry up. He must have been reminded of the incident at the Red Sea when the Israelites made their escape from Pharaoh's army over the dry seabed. Then some forty years later the writer of Joshua recorded another such incident: "And the priests who carried the ark of the covenant of the Lord stood firm on dry ground in the middle of the

Jordan while all Israel crossed on dry ground, until all the nation had finished crossing the Jordan" (Joshua 3:17, NASB).

Both Isaiah and Jeremiah make reference to God's action in drying up waters, and Zechariah writes about the Lord drying up the mighty Nile River in Egypt (Zechariah 10:11). These all speak of God's power at work in nature to achieve His eternal purposes.

But now this direct reference to the drying up of the Euphrates River was a judgment that would have frightened the people of Rome. You recall in our explanation of the vision of the sixth angel with the trumpet beginning with verse 13 of chapter 9 that there were two hundred million barbarians amassed on the other side of the Euphrates ready to march on Rome. The dreaded Parthians who had defied Rome's might would now be free to cross into the eastern reaches of the Roman Empire on the dry bed of the Euphrates.

Then, too, you'll remember in our earlier discussion the mention of the popular myth of that time in which it was thought mad Emperor Nero had been revived from his suicide attempt and had escaped to Parthia east of the Euphrates. It was believed Nero would return as the head of a Parthian army and conquer the Roman Empire. This was a judgment that would turn any Roman's knees to jelly.

### Unclean Spirits, the False Prophet, and Armageddon

Again, we are confronted with strange images that are revolting to our sensitivities. Out of the mouth of the "dragon"—the one in charge of promoting caesar worship, as we saw earlier, come "three unclean spirits like frogs" (16:13, KJV). John intended the frogs to convey an evil sense of revulsion since in many world religions frogs symbolize bad or sinister forces. These unclean creatures carry out the wishes of Satan, the dragon, in his attempt to induce worship of Rome and caesar. The "unclean spirits like frogs" are indeed a sinister trinity of evil that were even capable of doing so-called miracles as a way to convince people of their might and influence.

Verse 13 gives us our first mention of the false prophet. This mysterious one is mentioned in just two other places in the book of Revelation (19:20 and 20:10). As we piece together these references, it would seem that this false prophet is one whose mission is to convince people to worship caesar and other false gods.

Before going on with this strange scene, it is important to underline the truth that such a false prophet and unclean spirits are not peculiar to John's vision or to the latter part of the first century. These are present with us today, although we see them in less grotesque forms.

Outwardly, our false gods have a much less revolting form, but inwardly they are just as destructive. We worship power, money, prestige, friends, family, our vocation. Anything that takes first place in our lives is a god. In contrast to the unsightly images in John's vision, our twenty-first-century images take on a definite aura of respectability, and that is what makes them doubly dangerous.

This is precisely why we do well to understand this part of John's vision, because we get a picture here in verse 14 that these godless powers under the leadership of Satan, the evil one, are marshaling their forces for the "battle of that great day of God Almighty" (KJV). In other words, the vision looks to a time when the forces of God and the forces of Satan are locked in conflict.

Many have said, "War is hell." And in this scene in John's vision, we see hell about to break loose in what is referred to as Armageddon.

Before going on with his description of what will happen when the forces of God and of Satan are locked in combat, John interjects a parenthetical statement (which some translations set off in actual parentheses) in which we have a message from Christ to the Christians in the seven churches and in all time. "(Behold, I am coming like a thief! Blessed is the one who stays awake, keeping his garments on, that he may not go about naked and be seen exposed!)" (16:15, ESV).

The warning is clear. In spite of all attempts at speculation, we don't know when Jesus will come again and introduce a whole new time. We need only know that Jesus will come unannounced—"like a thief." The important thing is to remain alert and prepared so we'll not be ashamed or embarrassed in any way because of something we are doing or not doing. In His colorful parable-story of the servants and the ten pounds, Jesus specifically instructed them to "engage in business until I come" (Luke 19:13, ESV). That is our task as Christians—and to engage in business means to actively use the gifts and resources God has given us, participate in what is going on, and understand what we are to do about it.

Now, with the end of the brief parenthesis, John writes, "Then they gathered the kings together to the place that in Hebrew is called Armageddon" (16:16, NIV). Here the evil powers of Satan and this world are confronted by the armies of the Lord—a long-expected battle between the forces of evil and the forces of God that is inevitable.

The word Armageddon is literally translated "Hill of Megiddo." The reference is quite likely to that ancient battle-ground located on the Plain of Esdraelon. Any reader of the Old Testament would have caught the significance of the use of this name. It was a place of great tragedy. King Necho of Egypt had fought King Josiah there, and Israel's greatest king since David was killed (2 Kings 23:29).

Following Josiah's death, Judah's fortunes plunged straight downhill. In less than thirty years the southern kingdom of Judah was plundered by King Nebuchadnezzar of Babylon, and a few pitiful survivors were herded into exile a thousand miles away.

Megiddo, some sixty miles north of Jerusalem, near Mount Carmel, became a grim symbol of the battlefield of nations. It has rightly come down into the imagination of our century as the setting for the great battle between Christ and the counter-christ. Politicians, novelists, and moviemakers have made the most of this imagery.

And so as John has recorded his vision, we catch a subtle portrayal for his original readers and for us that the "new Babylon"—the Roman Empire—will feel God's judgment at the very place where the old Babylon was victorious. But Armageddon as portrayed in this vision is bigger than the judgment of Roman tyranny. The larger picture is seen in the ultimate destruction of Satan and his forces of evil by the Lamb of God—Jesus Christ.

We see in this scene the triumph of good over evil. This is the great Good News in this part of our lesson. As members of God's family, we have complete assurance that God is in charge of everything that happens to us in this life as well as in the one to come.

## The Seventh Judgment—the End

John tells us that "the seventh angel poured out his bowl upon the air" (16:17, NASB). The air, essential to all life, was attacked by this plague. In his vision John saw and felt thunder, lightning, voices, and an earthquake that exceeded anything seen or felt in that first century (16:18). This was the great cataclysmic happening that destroyed "Babylon"— Rome—the symbol of Satan's whole structure and human-kind's demon-driven pride.

Verses 20 and 21 give us a picture of devastating judgment and destruction capped off with deadly hailstones of unbelievable size. Once again the destructiveness of hail has its roots in Old Testament history. It struck Egypt before the Exodus as one of the plagues. In one of Israel's battles under Joshua we're told that more of the enemy soldiers were killed by hailstones than by any other way. And it becomes a weapon of God's judgment in Ezekiel 38:22. All of this would undoubtedly have been pictured and understood by John's first readers.

## A Final Reflection

There is much in this awesome scene with its strange and vivid imagery that can puzzle and confuse us. Our pragmatic twenty-first-century Western minds are just not very well equipped to wrestle with apocalyptic writing and first-century codes.

But as we reflect on John's amazing visions in this lesson, we're left almost speechless at the majesty of our God. Then, too, we've seen that as the Creator of all the universe, He is in charge of what happens. Nothing is beyond His ultimate control. But what is so astounding is that this same God is also our heavenly Father. This is mind-boggling as we reach for the challenge of living each twenty-four-hour day as witnesses of our Lord to everyone we meet.

For the Christian with this kind of God, life is full of adventure. It is upbeat. Ours isn't a gloom-and-doom faith; it's a resurrection faith!

John's visions in our lesson also give us proof positive of the triumph of good over evil. Yes, Christians of every century have been plagued by war and hunger and evil of every kind imaginable. Our years are colored by the evil forces of terrorism, nuclear danger, hunger, unbridled technology, and wars large and small. We're uneasy about traveling in certain places for fear of zealots and madmen who want to make their point by taking hostages and killing.

Every century has had its Rome, and ours is no different. But John's message for us in this lesson is that good does prevail over evil. God is patient in that He wants all people to have the opportunity to repent and claim His salvation (1 Peter 3:9). But the time is coming when evil will meet its final defeat, when God's love and justice will win out over all forms of opposition.

Of this great truth we can be sure. And our challenge is to live in victory every day of our lives. This is the word of the Lord.

*Our Father, there are times that challenge my belief in Your sovereignty. In times of suffering, I'm tempted to wonder. How I need to know that Your sovereignty isn't gauged by how well it goes with me. You are yet in control, completely and unequivocally. Help me always stand on Your solid Rock of assurance. "All other ground is sinking sand." AMEN.*

# SARDIS

Sardis, the fifth church John wrote to, was approximately thirty miles south and slightly east of Thyatira. It was this church that received a warning against apathy and indifference. The Temple of Artemis in Sardis was the chief pagan temple of the city and probably the most impressive building in the city at the time of John's writing.

# Notes

# *Notes*

# The Collapse of Evil— God's Victory

*Lord, victory has been a consistent theme in these lessons. You have already attained it—help me to fully receive it. Permeate my life with Your victory—for Your glory.* AMEN.

In the last scene of lesson 6, John described how Rome— the personification of all that was evil—was crushed by the shattering earthquake and the rain of huge hailstones. Our lesson now opens as one of the seven angels leads John to another stage and a different scene. Here John witnesses the fall of Rome a second time, this time in a sort of slow motion sequence and in greater detail.

As a matter of fact, John devotes more space to the description of this climactic event than to anything else. From our twenty-first-century vantage point we might well wonder why this is so—why it was so important to John and those first readers.

The details of John's vision about God's judgment on the city of Rome were of great importance to those first-century Christians. They were intimately familiar with the evils that characterized society in the Roman world. There was no place for what they and we understand as decency, a respect for human values and life, and moral responsibility. Caesar worship and worship of pagan gods had plunged Roman society into all forms of moral disintegration. And the brutal and sadistic persecution of Christians who insisted upon obedience first to God unleashed a bloodbath of horrendous proportions.

In other words, to John and his readers Rome represented all that was evil in the world. Rome was the archenemy of God and of all forces for good. Yet to a first-century Christian, Rome seemed invincible. The empire was riding high in the world. In the mood of the traditional American western movie, Rome, with its "black hat," was the winner in every encounter; those in the "white hats"—the people of God—were the losers. And from all reasonable and practical appearances there didn't seem to be anything that could change the picture.

## The Fall of Rome (17:1–18)

This is why in the wisdom of God John was given this "replay" vision in detail of the destruction of Rome—of evil. In this graphic picture of flaming destruction, we see the ultimate victory of God over Satan and over all forces of evil. Yes, they had been allowed to exist for a time, and yes, the sadistic caesars and their henchmen appeared to have their own way. But God in His patience was giving humankind the time and opportunity to repent. However, those early Christians who were suffering intense persecution needed this assurance and reassurance that in spite of the way things looked, God was in charge. The sinister powers of Satan were not winning out. God's judgment would be felt at the proper moment on first-century Rome.

But as our eyes now focus on the destructive scene of Rome's demise, we don't see an angry and vengeful God at work in the world. He wasn't "out to get" Rome. Instead, He was trying to rescue her people even though they seemed set on self-destruction. Tragically, the Roman people had made a conscious decision to reject Jesus Christ, and now they were forced to endure the consequences of their decision.

### Babylon, the Harlot

Now, let's move in and take a close look at what John saw next. The angel, in directing his attention to a new scene, said, "'Come here, I will show you the judgment of the great prostitute who sits on many waters'" (17:1, NASB). In the opening words of our scripture lesson (17:1–6) the prostitute is identified as Babylon, the code word for Rome. And we see in these descriptive words John's use of symbolism at its best.

It is true in verse 1 that the identification of Babylon with Rome is a bit blurred because of its location by "many waters." This seems to apply to ancient Babylon and not to Rome. But this is cleared up in verse 15 where it is explained that "waters" is a symbolic term for the many nations under Rome's rule.

As we take in this bizarre scene John describes, we see a scarlet-colored beast, symbolic of the vast Roman Empire. Riding the beast is the "whore" (KJV), the city of Rome. Outwardly, we see her gaudy splendor. Our first view pictures her in all of her power and glory (17:4), but beneath this glittery façade are the "abominations and filthiness of her fornication" (KJV). She is the personification of evil and she is supported by Satan, who is the real power behind the empire.

To heighten the revulsion in this scene, John writes, "I saw that the woman was drunk with the blood of God's holy people, the blood of those who bore testimony to Jesus. When I saw her, I was greatly astonished" (17:6, NIV). Here we have a graphic picture of an evil city that was drunk with the slaughter of Christians in the city's arenas.

It is difficult if not impossible for us in our time to imagine the sadistic cruelty of that late first-century persecution of Christians, but Tacitus, the Roman historian, writes that "even for criminals who deserved extreme and exemplary punishment, there arose a feeling of compassion [for the Christians], for it was not, as it seemed, for the public good, but to glut one man's cruelty that they were being destroyed."

Perhaps no better description than "harlot" could be found for Rome. The worship of Rome and of Emperor Domitian held the empire together in a seductive embrace. It was a society satiated by evil influences. Seneca, noted Roman writer and philosopher of that period, referred to the city as "a filthy sewer."

All of this is to emphasize the significance of the imagery in this scene. The Roman prostitutes of the first century shaved their heads and wore headbands bearing the letter *P* for *porne*—prostitute. The one John saw wore a more elaborate inscription (17:5). But the identification was important for John's readers. In the Old Testament, idolatry is equated with harlotry and was loathed by God and His people. This was

Rome of the late first century. This was the Rome John and his readers knew.

### *The Mystery of "Babylon"*

Following this amazing scene, which must have left John almost speechless, the angel returns and says, "'I will tell you the mystery of the woman, and of the beast with seven heads and ten horns that carries her'" (17:7, ESV). Now comes the explanation, and again, it is in code. This explanation needed to come through in an understandable way to those first-century Christian readers, but it should remain incomprehensible to anyone else. In other words, had this book fallen into the hands of the Roman authorities, it would have been meaningless—yet the Christians knew exactly what was meant. There may be times when we will feel a bit like a first-century Roman as we read these mysterious words.

What the angel is going to do now is let John see the real picture, not just the external scene. He will see "the scene behind the scene."

First, our attention is focused on the beast as John writes, "The beast that you saw was [once], but [now] is not, and he is about to come up out of the abyss (the bottomless pit, the dwelling place of demons) and go to destruction (perdition)" (17:8, AMP). The beast, of course, is Satan, the center of the real power of evil. The rider, the prostitute—Rome—is only a mistress or tool of Satan and is entirely dependent on him.

Satan, as a pseudo-god, is said here to have a four-fold career: he "was, and is not, and is about to rise from the bottomless pit and go to destruction" (17:8, ESV). This is in sharp contrast to the four-fold career of Christ, in which He lived, died, rose again, and ascended into heaven and lives forever. It is because of Jesus Christ that we Christians are able to see through Satan's deceptions and avoid being trapped.

Second, John was shown the meaning of Satan's power in the symbol of the beast's seven heads (verse 9) and the ten horns (verse 12). These are symbolic of Satan's authority. The "seven mountains" (verse 9) are, of course, a reference to Rome, which was built on seven hills. But more is involved than a geographic reference as we reach for the deeper insight that implies authority, solidarity, and strength.

Also, in true apocalyptic style, we have the reference to the "seven kings," which is symbolic of political power. The city of Rome was indeed the home of the mighty caesars who ruled the empire. Those caesars have had their counterparts in every century. Unfortunately, godless governments didn't stop with the early caesars. The steps of history have given us our Genghis Kahns, Napoleons, Hitlers, Saddam Husseins, and Pol Pots.

A link can even be seen between the seven kings and the seven caesars who had reigned up to that time as a means of pointing to the final doom of Satan. This comparison was carefully done so as to avoid charges of sedition. The imagery is disguised so that insiders would understand but outsiders wouldn't. Most certainly the identification of the king who "is not yet come" (KJV) refers to the legend already described whereby Nero would return reincarnated in Domitian—a mad murderer as vicious as Nero (17:10).

Third, John's attention is drawn to the ten horns or ten kings "who have not yet received a kingdom, but who for one hour will receive authority as kings along with the beast" (17:12, NIV). These "kings" are likely puppet rulers within the empire and are also symbolic of political power. It would seem that these rulers had formed an uneasy alliance with Rome but would ultimately be unfaithful to the ungodly city and turn against her. Allies like these find their modern counterpart in political or religious opportunists who out of self-interest become part of an alliance, but who abandon the movement the moment their purposes are served. These, too, will arrive at their moment of judgment.

Fourth, in verses 16 and 17, John was given a look into the distant future where the evil ones have a falling-out among themselves. You've heard the cliché about "honor among thieves," but there was no honor among these "kings." Throughout the centuries of time selfishness among nations has been the pattern even as it was in Roman times. Evil linked with evil produces fickle allies.

During the Second World War, Hitler and Stalin signed a pact of agreement on Poland. But it wasn't long before Hitler launched his secret attack on Russia, his supposed ally. Again, it was a case in which circumstances and events weren't always the way they looked. In this we, too, can take comfort. Even in our time, the forces of evil can and do turn on themselves.

Finally, the angel told John that "the woman that you saw is the great city that has dominion over the kings of the earth" (17:18, ESV). With this, the identity is solidified. Rome, the great imperial city with its magnificent buildings, its pomp, and its glory, had chosen to follow false gods. To remain faithful to this first-century epitome of evil was both sin and false patriotism. Its doom was assured.

During the American Civil War, President Lincoln remarked that he was not as concerned about God being on his side as he was that he was on God's side, "for God is always right." The challenge for us as Christian citizens in the twenty-first century is to remember that our primary allegiance is to God. It is God we worship, not the state, and not human leaders. It is God we serve.

And so we have in this vision the prediction of Rome's fall in spite of her civil religion. She would collapse from rottenness within long before the final chapter was written by the Germanic barbarians who crossed the Alps and plundered the country.

## The Fall of Rome Foretold (18:1–3)

John's visions continue now with the appearance of another angel who speaks with powerful poetic imagery and announces that "Babylon the great is fallen" (18:2, KJV). While that event was yet in the future, it is referred to here as an accomplished fact. At this time of writing, the city of Rome was powerful and attractive even though it was menacing. But its inner core was being rotted out even though that couldn't be seen. The point is clear: Rome's repression would not be permanent. The "everlasting hills" of Rome were not everlasting. The end was so certain it was an accomplished fact. God's judgments are sure.

## Practical Instructions for Roman Christians (18:4-8)

Another voice moves on to center stage with instructions: "Come out of her, my people, so that you will not participate in her sins and receive any of her plagues" (18:4, NASB). Christians were warned not to be involved in Rome's sins and excesses. They were to be different and were to sever any relationship with surrounding evil.

In verse 5 we are told that Rome's sins are stacked as high as heaven, but in verse 6 we read that God's judgment will be commensurate with the sin. Nevertheless, Roman citizens remain self-confident and arrogant as they say, "'I sit enthroned as queen. I am not a widow; I will never mourn'" (18:7, NIV). Governments then and now are instinctively proud and selfish, but Christians are warned against that trap.

The people of Rome were guilty of inflated egos, of unparalleled insolence. They were convinced they didn't need God. This was the mood at Ur when God instructed Abraham to move out. Throughout all of history, believers in God have been instructed to separate themselves from any identification of evil.

We dare not become soft and comfortable in our Christian pilgrimage. There's no room for either comfort or insolence in our church life. Instead we are to be vigorous in our stand for the right in all areas of our lives. And in contrast to the Roman attitude, the Christian citizen can never say, "My country, right or wrong." Instead, we can pray, "My country: when in the right, keep it right; when in the wrong, put it right."

# Rome's Allies Grieve Over Her Fall (18:9-20)

The vision continues, and we are now treated to the colorful picture of how three specific groups of people react to the fall and destruction of Rome: the kings of the earth (18:9-10); the merchants of the earth (18:11-16); and "every sea captain, and all who travel by ship, the sailors, and all who earn their living from the sea" (18:17-19, NIV).

### *The Grief of Kings and Rulers*

Naturally those petty rulers and government leaders who had profited by their association with Rome were grieved to see their benefactor destroyed (18:9-10). But it would seem that their concern was only because the goose that had been laying golden eggs for them was dead. Other than that, they had no loyalty or interest. Their lament was phony as they stood "afar off for the fear of her torment" (18:10, KJV).

In other words, Rome's friends among the kings and rulers associated with her were really fair-weather friends. There was no depth or quality to the relationships because they were based solely on selfish gain. This stands in vivid contrast to authentic Christian friendships and alliances. And the difference is in motive. Rome's alliances were based on what each party could *get* from the other. Christian alliances and friendships are based on what we can *give* in mutual sharing.

So, yes, neighboring kings and rulers grieved because of what they had lost, and they stood "afar off" in fear.

## The Merchants of the Earth

Now, this group of rascals who had traded their wares with Rome, the business capital of the world, were even more heartless than their political friends (18:11–16). Their only reason for weeping and mourning over Rome's fall was because "no one buys their cargo anymore" (18:11, ESV). Only their greed and profit motive prompted grief. And now they would have to go out and find a new market.

In verses 12 and 13 John lists twenty-eight luxury items that were traded with Rome, and the last item listed was slaves. To them, human bodies were merchandise to be bought and sold. It was a heartless system, and they were heartless people. But, again, their form of insensitivity was not restricted to the first century.

*Roots*, both the book and the two television mini-series adaptations, reminded us how heartless our own system of slavery was. A museum displayed a will from the early 1800s that listed the property a man had bequeathed to his heirs. Among them was one piece of merchandise "named Isaac, thirteen years old." Further research indicated that Isaac had been an enslaved person who worked in the household. Here was a boy, created in the image of God, who was offered in the marketplace as a commodity.

Many of John's readers were enslaved people or formerly enslaved, and they would certainly have seen the irony in the merchants' "grief." And, of course, the lesson here is clear. Alliances and friendships based only on "bottom line" profits are thin. Such are a part of a worldly system and have little or nothing to do with basic life values.

### Shipmasters and Sailors

The third group that "cried out when they saw the smoke of her burning" were those who sailed the Mediterranean in ships loaded down with valuable cargo headed for Ostia, the port of Rome (18:17–19, ESV). As with the others, their "weeping and wailing" (KJV) was only because a market for their goods had disappeared: "Alas, alas, for the great city where all who had ships at sea grew rich by her wealth!" (ESV).

As mighty as Rome had been over the centuries of her greatness, John's visions looked ahead to that time when her rubble would join that of other great cities of the past. The good news was that Christ would outlast the Roman caesars even as He will the "caesars" of all time. The message to the seven churches was clear. They had chosen the way of righteousness that would lead to ultimate victory; corrupt Rome would receive its reward in ruin, and no one would mourn its passing except those with greedy self-interest.

### What Does This Mean to Me?

What does this sad panorama of destruction mean to us as we attempt to live for Christ in a very real now? What can we take away from this scene that will make us better people and help us grow in our Christian faith?

These are good questions. Yes, the book of Revelation is written in a form and style that is strange to us. But it is an important part of our Bible, and it isn't a closed book. In the midst of the picture language and code words there are practical lessons for us.

First, John's descriptions of what he saw and heard underline the eternal truth that because God is a God of love, justice will prevail. Sixty million people cannot be enslaved in a vicious system without a cataclysmic payoff. Human beings cannot be turned into torches or clawed apart in coliseums by ferocious animals without their tormentors being confronted by a God of justice. Those who deliberately harm and kill can't get away with it, whether in Rome or Auschwitz or Aleppo.

But there's another side to the coin. God's justice will have its day for those who assassinate the characters of their fellow human beings for personal gain or who by unfair means of competition ruin the life and business of another person. To claw one's way up the "success" ladder by shoving others aside is a vicious, destructive game seen all too frequently in our everyday life. And to spread gossip and put down another person as a means of building ourselves up is an outrageous wrong whether it happens in business, at the country club, or in church. A God of love and justice moves in society to right all such forms of tyranny.

Second, we can learn how God reveals His character within the framework of history. Rome was a real place, and the Christians in the seven churches in the province of Asia were real people. All that happened during those early years of the Christian church and in society was not the invention of a novelist or short-story writer. These were real events in real time.

Third, as we reflect on the meaning of what John saw, we see that what God revealed about Himself in these judgment narratives has a timeless relevance that applies to our lives today. There's more here than the story of Rome's corrupt and brutal lifestyle and of the city's destruction. But we are to learn from this dramatic story that to misuse power and material resources has its inevitable cost. What is right, what is fair and just, is the ultimate winner in the drama of human events. To violate that eternal principle is to invite disaster.

## Rome—A Ghost Town (18:21-24)

Now we see the total ruin of Rome and all that it stood for as John writes about what he saw next: "Then a strong angel picked up a stone like a great millstone and threw it into the sea, saying, 'So will Babylon, the great city, be thrown down with violence, and will never be found again'" (18:21, NASB). These words and description are reminiscent of what the prophet Jeremiah had to say about the ruin and destruction of ancient Babylon, the archetype of Rome (Jeremiah 51:62–64).

These verses give us a colorful description of the silence and blackness that hovered over the fallen city. The silence was deafening—no sounds of people working, or music, not even "the voice of the bridegroom and of the bride" (18:23, KJV) could be heard. There was silence and darkness and death. God's judgment could be seen throughout the entire world. Yes, we can visit a bustling twenty-first-century Rome, but it is a different city than the one seen in this part of John's vision.

## A Celebration in Heaven (19:1-5)

With the destruction of Rome and with the victory of God over the forces of evil, all of those in heaven break out into a great hallelujah chorus of praise to God.

For the Christian, an attitude of hallelujah and praise is meant to be a part of every moment. Yes, we have our hard times and our moments of trial, but our "Romes" have been defeated by our Lord at Calvary and the empty tomb. The Domitians, the Stalins, and the Hitlers of our world don't have the last word—God does. And so we say with that great heavenly chorus that John saw and heard, "Praise the Lord!"

This celebration of praise provides a model for our time even as it was for those early Christians. Often, far too much of our God-directed attention is focused on our wants and needs. Beyond that we tend to take God for granted. But the "praise Christian" has caught the spirit of this heavenly choir, and it is this spirit that makes the Good News appealing to those who do not know Christ.

## An Invitation to Dine (19:6–10)

The hymn of praise continues now as John writes that he "heard what sounded like a great multitude, like the roar of rushing waters and like loud peals of thunder, shouting: 'Hallelujah! For our Lord God Almighty reigns. Let us rejoice and be glad and give him glory! For the wedding of the Lamb has come, and his bride has made herself ready" (19:6–7, NIV). Again, the imagery is rich as we understand that the Lamb, of course, is Jesus Christ, and the bride is His church. The metaphor of marriage as characterizing the relationship of God's people with Him is expressed frequently in both the Old and New Testaments.

The prophet Isaiah expresses this idea beautifully as he writes, "For your Maker is your husband, the LORD of hosts is his name; and the Holy One of Israel is your Redeemer, the God of the whole earth he is called" (Isaiah 54:5, ESV). A number of such references appear in the Gospels, including Jesus's parable of the marriage supper (Matthew 22:1–10). And Paul makes use of this same metaphor several times, including his powerful statement about the relationship of Christ and His church in Ephesians 5:22–33.

Here in these verses the people of God, the bride, are pictured as being clothed "in fine linen, bright and clean; for the fine linen is the righteous acts of the saints" (19:8, NASB). Note the difference in the description of the bride's attire as compared to that of the harlot mentioned earlier. Here we see a purified and holy church ready for its union with Christ the Lord.

The magnificent beauty and pageantry of this scene was almost more than John could handle, for he writes, "At this I fell at his feet to worship him" (19:10, NIV), though the angel immediately tells him not to do so. The Christians in the seven churches who first received this message from John's hand must have been equally stunned. Their present fate must have seemed very dark. Persecution and oppression rested heavily upon them like an enormous weight, but this glimpse into their future as the bride of Christ—His chosen one— would have inspired enormous hope.

But this is our future too—yours and mine. Yes, even with all our imperfections Christ is with us in our daily tussle with life. But we, too, can look ahead to that time when our imperfections are made perfect and we are united with Christ.

## The Victorious Christ (19:11–16)

Next John's attention is shifted from the scene of the heavenly chorus and the marriage supper as he writes that "heaven opened, and behold, a white horse, and He who sat on it is called Faithful and True, and in righteousness He judges and wages war" (19:11, NASB). And the description of the rider that follows in verses 12 through 16 defies comparison.

Such drama and color! The white horse was the symbol of victory, and a familiar sight to Roman citizens as they watched their generals in victory parades. As John's apocalyptic imagery reaches new heights, we see Christ as the final victory over Satan and all forces of evil. The splendor of His appearance authenticates His victory. And then to make certain there is no doubt as to His identity, we're told in verse 16 that engraved on His robe were the words "KING OF KINGS, AND LORD OF LORDS" (NASB).

This is our Savior!

## The Judgment of the Forces of Evil (19:17–21)

We come now to a grisly scene of judgment and carnage. Again, we have apocalyptic imagery at its most colorful. The forces of Satan are completely routed. And we see in verse 20 a repeat of the imagery in Revelation 13: the beast, Domitian; the false prophet, the state religion of caesar worship; those who had received the "mark of the beast," worshippers of caesar—all of these were consigned to "a lake of fire that burns with sulfur" (ESV). This "lake of fire" reference would have been readily recognized by John's first readers as the place of punishment—Gehenna, the ever-burning garbage dump outside the city of Jerusalem that symbolized hell.

## Christian Victory—Satan Is Bound (20:1-3)

We come now to the closing scene in our lesson. John saw another angel who had "the key to the Abyss and holding in his hand a great chain. He seized the dragon, that ancient serpent, who is the devil, or Satan, and bound him for a thousand years" (20:1-2, NIV).

With the binding of Satan, Christ's victory is complete. This climactic step would have greatly encouraged those first-century readers. Harried as they were on all sides, now they are told that the evil one is shut up and sealed for a thousand years!

The periods of time mentioned in Revelation have been interpreted in different ways over the years. But this thousand-year period needs to be viewed in connection with two other such references in our Bible. The Psalmist wrote, "For a thousand years in Your sight are like yesterday when it passes by, or like a watch in the night" (Psalm 90:4, NASB). Another such reference is found in 2 Peter 3:8, "But, beloved, be not ignorant of this one thing, that one day is with the Lord as a thousand years, and a thousand years as one day" (KJV). While, of course, there is much about all of this of which we can't be certain, it is likely from these companion references that the term "a thousand years" refers to a long period of time. The important thing is that Satan is bound; God is in control, and during this period of time the Christian saints who had suffered martyrdom will reign with their Lord.

At the very end of our scripture lesson, John writes that after this thousand-year period Satan will be freed for a short time. Again, we can't be absolutely certain about what is meant here, but it is thought that Satan is loosed for a short time to test the faithfulness of the Christians to make sure that none had become lax during the thousand-year period that Satan was bound.

## A Closing Comment

Our journey together through John's visions and the pictures in these three chapters has been full of strange sights and sounds. To our twenty-first-century literal and pragmatic understanding much of the description boggles our minds. We're not accustomed to first-century images and apocalyptic visions. But throughout this part of our study, we have been attentive to the Word of the Lord.

What do we take from this? Certainly not the thought that God has given us some sort of heavenly calendar of time and events. What we have seen is a patient God at work in our world.

Yes, the forces of evil have been loose in the world since the beginning of time. And it is true that as we view events through our finite lenses, it may seem those forces are in control. But the good news for us through these visions of John is that God's clock is the accurate measurement of time and that our future as daughters and sons of the Lord is secure. Furthermore, our hope is fixed in the absolute assurance that God is in charge of all He has made.

With that confidence we can lock our arms with Christians of all time and sing, "We shall overcome," in and through Jesus Christ.

"Hallelujah! For the Lord our God the Almighty reigns" (19:6, ESV).

*Father, help me be alert to the pilgrimage aspect of my Christian life. Let me be fully here, yet always fully aware that this is only my temporary home. In Jesus's name,* AMEN.

# SMYRNA

Modern Ismir, Turkey, was the site of ancient Smyrna, the second of the seven churches. Smyrna was located northeast of Ephesus, approximately forty-one miles away. A major city of the province of Asia, it is estimated the population was between 100,000 and 200,000 at the time John wrote.

# *Notes*

# *Notes*

# The Christian's Eternal Destiny: The New Heaven and Earth

◆————————————————◆

*Lord, let this lesson come alive for me. It's a real privilege to gain an understanding of my eternal destiny, and of Your new heaven and earth.* AMEN.

I n our studies John has been moving us along steadily toward that time of final victory for Christians. He has shown us how the alliance of evil—Satan and his forces— was thoroughly defeated. He has also reviewed for us how Christians were robbed, persecuted, put in concentration camps, and murdered. Then, in our last lesson we moved on in John's visions and saw the fall of Rome and her allies, how the city was turned into a burned-over rubble, how the "beast" and the "false prophet" were thrown into the pit, and that Satan was chained in the bottomless pit for a thousand years.

This scenario of the ultimate defeat of Satan and the forces of evil was important to the late first-century Christians who were suffering intensely for their faith. There was just no way they could handle the present without assurance of the ultimate defeat of evil. And so we see that it was this assurance

John could give them because of what he had seen and heard in the visions.

## Victory with the Martyrs: the Millennium (20:4-10)

### The "Losers" Are Winners

From all outward appearances those Christians who had been slaughtered by Emperor Domitian and his predecessors were the losers of history. But now as John's vision moved from the bottomless pit toward heaven, he saw something new, and he shares this with those who are still alive in the seven churches. He saw on thrones "souls of those who had been beheaded because of their testimony of Jesus and because of the word of God, and those who had not worshipped the beast or his image, and had not received the mark on their foreheads and on their hands; and they came to life and reigned with Christ for a thousand years" (20:4, NASB).

### The Golden Age of "One Thousand Years"

In other words, what we see here is that these "losers"—those who had been killed for their faith in Christ alone—have been resurrected and are now overcomers and rule with Christ for "a thousand years." At various places Satan's time in this world is pictured as symbolically short—"three and one-half years," "three and one-half days," "one hour," "a little season." Compared with Satan's limited tenure, the martyrs and their Lord were to be in charge for a very long period of time.

Evil's triumph had been comparatively brief, but this triumph over evil would continue for a wonderfully long time. The contrast must have been spine-tingling for the beleaguered Christians of the late first century.

The idea of a Golden Age was firmly entrenched in John's background of Judaism. The apocalyptic writers saw it in different ways—forty, sixty, seventy, one hundred, one thousand, two thousand, or seven thousand years. However long the reign of the Messiah, the triumph of all that was right and good was greatly anticipated. The symbolism is rich in its depiction of victory and fulfillment under the righteous reign of Jesus Christ. Evil was defeated; goodness prevailed, and those who had suffered so greatly were now living in victory.

John devotes only a few words of description to these thousand years of time, but this in no way minimizes their truth and promise of hope. To the faithful Christian of all times— good as well as bad—the promise of the complete victory of God over evil gives us an incomparable hope.

### The First Resurrection

Now in verses 5 and 6 we learn in a parenthetical note that "(The rest of the dead did not come to life until the thousand years were ended)" (NIV). And for these "the second death has no power over them" (NIV). Different interpretations of "the first resurrection" have existed over the centuries, as they have for the meaning of the "thousand years." Such differences appeared very early in the life of the church and continue to this present day.

For some, the first resurrection refers to those who suffered death for their faith—the martyrs. Then there are those who hold to the idea that it refers to our conversion to Christ—our passing from death to life. But the central idea in these verses is that in that future world the wrongs that have existed in this world will be righted, and that as Christians we can be assured of eternal life with Christ in the world to come.

## The Final Battle

Now, in these next verses the scene shifts again (20:7–10). The thousand-year period is over, and as was mentioned earlier, Satan is released for a time. He brings together all of his forces in one last effort to defeat the Christians. John writes that the number of this vast army of evil was "as the sand of the sea" (20:8, KJV). You will notice these evil forces are referred to in our scripture lesson as Gog and Magog. This identification had special meaning for the Jew because of the prophet's writing in Ezekiel 38 and 39. Again, over the centuries the identity of Gog and Magog has been consigned to many different nations. But the likely reference here is to any and all forces that are arrayed against God.

## God Intervenes

But this last battle becomes no battle at all because John next sees that "fire came down from heaven and consumed them [the forces of evil]" (20:9, ESV). And then in verse 10 the imagery takes on bizarre proportions again as John writes, "And the devil who had deceived them was thrown into the lake of fire and sulfur where the beast and the false prophet were, and they will be tormented day and night forever and ever" (ESV). And with this, God's triumph over Satan and evil is finalized!

### An Encouraging Word

What great good news this had to be to the Christians in the Asian churches and in all of the churches throughout the Roman Empire—Satan, the mad caesars, the cult of caesar worship, and evil of all kinds were no longer to be feared. Yes, they would have to go on living in their real world, and some of them might yet have to die for their faith, but they could do this knowing that future victory was certain.

And this is good news to us also. As followers of the Lord, we are always under siege from the forces of evil. "Gog and Magog" are very much alive and active in our world. Their form may be different than it was in the first century, but the effect is just as real. The temptations that confront us in our sophisticated and high-tech society are subtle and threatening, *but our security is in God.*

It is tragic that there need be a "lake of fire"—a second death, a place of eternal absence from God and all that is good, a place where there is no love. That is what hell is.

## The Final Judgment—the Great White Throne (20:11–15)

### The Place of Judgment

We come now to an awesome scene—a scene of judgment in which all of humankind assemble before God to be judged. John writes, "And I saw a great white throne, and him that sat

on it, from whose face the earth and the heaven fled away"
(20:11, KJV).

Here we see God as the judge on His white throne—a
symbol of His purity and sovereignty and justice. It must have
been an awesome sight of divine majesty because "earth and
heaven fled away"—disappeared, vanished without leaving
any trace.

### The Books Are Opened

Next we read that "books were opened; and another book was
opened, which is the book of life; and the dead were judged
from the things which were written in the books, according to
their deeds" (20:12, NASB). Jewish theology taught that God
kept record books in which everyone's good and evil deeds
were recorded.

John's vision draws on this tradition, and he makes reference to two books in particular. The first contained a record
of everyone's actions or deeds. From this we get a picture of
the idea that as we move through each day of our life, we are
shaping our future. God is attentive to our conduct.

But then there's a second book, which John refers to as the
book of life. This will also be a familiar term to John's first
readers. Reference is made to such a book by Moses in Exodus 32:32. And the "book of the living" is mentioned again
in Psalm 69:28. In the New Testament Paul picks up on this
same idea in his letter to the Philippians when he speaks of his
"co-workers, whose names are in the book of life" (4:3, NIV).

It is this book that contains the names of the people of God
from all time—those who have lived in faith and obedience

to Him and His eternal purposes. Revelation 19:13 makes it clear that *everyone* will be judged by the record in these books. And we are judged by both the record of our actions and our faith in Jesus Christ, the Lamb. Here we see the delicate balance between grace and obedience. In verse 15 we read that those whose names do not appear in the book of life are condemned to eternal separation from God.

The important message for us here is that if we belong to Christ, we are exempt from the judgment. Jesus made this clear when He said, "Truly, truly, I say to you, whoever hears my word and believes him who sent me has eternal life. He does not come into judgment, but has passed from death to life" (John 5:24, ESV). Our being listed in the book of life will counteract the just accusations brought against us in the record of our actions and deeds. We belong to Christ. His obedience covers our sins, we are considered righteous because of His righteousness, and His power within us produces holiness acceptable to God. The point is that we produce good works because of God's gift of salvation to us.

## A Present Experience

The present for each of us is terribly important, for true life actually begins here and now, as does true death. To *live* is to be given the gift of fellowship with God; to die is to reject this gift and live in separation from Him. This underlines the importance of our present decisions and actions and allegiance.

Our present carries eternal consequences. And John shows us in this lesson that there is a finale in the sense that we move out into eternity either *in* Christ or *not in* Christ. If we are *in Christ*, we have already experienced all of death that we will ever know. On the other hand, if we are *out of Christ*, we are actually existing in a form of living death.

### The Second Death

Finally, then, John tells us that "Death and Hades were thrown into the lake of fire. This is the second death, the lake of fire" (20:14, ESV). Here we see death and hell destroyed. And then we have living death—"the second death"—existence separated from God and everything that can meaningfully be called life.

It is important for us to understand that God does not consign anyone to separation from Him. We make the choice. The last tribute that God pays to our freedom is to let us choose hell even when it is against His will for us. We're not puppets. Being with God in the next world or being separated from Him is our own decision.

## All Things Are New (21:1–4)

Turning now from a scene of judgment, death, and destruction, John sees a new and awesome sight. His breath must have caught in his throat with excitement. We feel it as he writes, "Then I saw a new heaven and a new earth, for the first heaven and the first earth had passed away, and the sea was no more. And I saw the holy city, new Jerusalem, coming down out of heaven from God, prepared as a bride adorned for her husband. And I heard a loud voice from the throne saying, 'Behold, the dwelling place of God is with man. He will dwell with them, and they will be his people, and God himself will be with them as their God. He will wipe away every tear from their eyes, and death shall be no more, neither shall there be mourning, nor crying, nor pain anymore, for the former things have passed away'" (21:1–4, ESV).

### A New Person in a New World

The new person in Christ needs a new world. And these four magnificent verses introduce three new things: a new creation, a new city, and a new relationship with God. Each of these three new things is briefly outlined here and then expanded upon in subsequent paragraphs.

### A New Creation

As in the rest of the book, the imagery here is rich. First, we read that John saw a new creation—a new heaven and earth. Since the old creation had been corrupted by humankind's sin, a new creation was necessary. And in this new one, the sea—the ancient symbol of evil, danger, and desolation— "was no more" (21:1, ESV)

### A New City

Second, John saw a new city, a recreated holy Jerusalem. The old Jerusalem had been the site of the stoning of the prophets and the crucifixion of Jesus. But the new one looked like a beautifully dressed bride.

### A New Relationship

Third, John saw God's presence among His people in a new way—God living with His people in His full glory. Here we see a marvelous fulfillment of the earlier words of two of God's great prophets, "My dwelling place also will be among them; and I will be their God, and they will be My people" (Ezekiel 37:27, NASB); and "They shall be my people, and I will be their God" (Jeremiah 32:38, KJV). In these verses we find a whole new relationship between God and His people. We see the end of death and sorrow and pain. What can we say except "Hallelujah!"?

## The New Creation—All Things New (21:5–8)

Then God said, "'Behold, I am making all things new'" (21:5, ESV). Even as by God's word the old creation came into existence (Genesis 1), so now by His word the new one appears. And in verse 6 when God says, "It is done!" it means that all He has predicted and promised so far has come to pass—the End Time has arrived.

Christian believers are now in the fullest sense the children of God (21:7). This name or designation, this promise of God is the greatest glory He has given us as His children. We are officially members of the family of God.

But then in verse 8 there is a final condemnation on the unfaithful and unbelieving spiritually dead people who have refused to serve and worship God. It's a revolting and unsavory list—the corrupt, liars, murderers, idolaters, and fornicators, to name a few.

It is utterly impossible for us to even begin to imagine what this new creation would be like. The idea of living in a world entirely free of any form of evil is mind-boggling. To imagine living without pain or disease or emotional hurt is beyond our imagination. The thought of living in a world of peace seems almost impossible to grasp.

No war. No kidnapping or taking of hostages. Imagine! People in Syria, Russia, Ukraine, developing nations, the United States—all living in peace with one another. This is the picture John is giving us of a new creation.

## The New City—A Description of the New Jerusalem (21:9–14)

Now John writes, "One of the seven angels who had the seven bowls full of the seven last plagues came and said to me, 'Come, I will show you the bride, the wife of the Lamb'" (21:9, NIV). We read earlier that it was one of these angels who took John into the wilderness to show him the harlot (Rome). Now, possibly this same angel takes him to the mountaintop to show him the bride. What wonderful irony!

### Who Is the Bride?
But who is this bride? She is the new city, the new Jerusalem. And who makes up this new city, this New Jerusalem? It is the church of God, Christians of all time. It is made up of those early Christians in the seven churches and Christians in all corners of the globe since Jesus's resurrection—in every country of the world. It is you and me. In mystical and religious

language, we Christians are the bride and Christ is the Bridegroom. Unthinkable! How can we possibly measure up? How can God get us, the bride-city, ready for the "wedding feast"?

John answers these questions with lively imagery. First, he writes that God gives the city light "like a very valuable stone, like a stone of crystal-clear jasper" (21:11, NASB). From this we see that God's presence lights up the city brilliantly. We live in the light of His Presence.

Second, God has provided walls and city gates—symbols of its security, its means of access, and its limits (21:12–14). Walls surrounding ancient cities were to provide protection. The gates offered entrance to anyone who wanted to come in.

And, third, the city had a sound foundation, "the twelve apostles of the Lamb (Christ)" (21:14, AMP). It was the apostles' truth rooted in the truth of Christ that was the foundation for the city—the church of God.

## The New City—A Description of the New Jerusalem (21:15–21)

Now John launches into some of his most colorful language as he describes the city. He tells us in very literal terms its shape, dimensions, and the materials out of which it was built, but he does this merely to suggest that its greatness is beyond measuring. We can tell from the words that John is more concerned with good symbolism than he is with mathematics.

First, we note that the city is foursquare, the shape of a cube. Square cities were not unusual in the earliest of times, such as Nineveh and Babylon. But the cube idea is something else; in ancient times a cube was the symbol of perfection. In ancient Israel, the altars in the tabernacle and temple were in the shape of a cube, as was that sacred area in Solomon's Temple known as the Holy of Holies. From this John wants us to see the perfection of the city, the church, as it assumes its rightful role as the place where God lives.

Second, we note with amazement the size of the city—fifteen hundred miles each way, two and one-quarter million square miles. This is most certainly symbolic of the truth that there is sufficient room for everybody who has professed allegiance in Christ.

You will notice in reading these verses the repeated use of the number twelve. This is no accident either. The number twelve represents perfection, wholeness, and completeness. It is large enough, spacious enough, to include everyone, and its walls symbolize the security of the believer in God's presence.

But it is the splendor of the building materials that defies any realistic description (21:18–21): jasper, gold, sapphires, diamonds, emeralds, agates, rubies, malachite, amethyst, pearls. This is a stunning and awesome picture of unparalleled beauty. From all of this we catch a faint glimmer of just how precious and important the church is to God.

## The New Relationship—God's Presence in New Jerusalem (21:22–27)

In the verses we've just studied, John's vision offers a startling view of the beauty and magnificence of the church—the people of God—in that place the Lord has provided for faithful

Christians in His new world, the new heaven and the new earth. Now in this part of our study his vision gives us a grand summary of the Good News—the divine message that brings us and keeps us in an intimate relationship with God. John's penetrating view here sees the actual fulfillment of his earlier words: "Behold, the tabernacle of God is with men, and *he will dwell with them, and they shall be his people, and God himself shall be with them*" (21:3, KJV, emphasis added). Now God is indeed with and among His people.

## No Need for a Temple

John writes, "And I saw no temple in the city, for its temple is the Lord God the Almighty and the Lamb" (21:22, ESV). From this we see that there was no longer a need for a special house of God. This would have been a shocker to the Jewish reader. The tabernacle and the temple had always been their place of meeting with God. This is where He had always promised He would meet His people. But now He is so intimately present with His people where they are that no special place of meeting is needed.

Here we have the wonderful fulfillment of the present truth that it isn't buildings or forms of worship or a special vocabulary that makes the church. Rather it is the presence of the living Christ. And John helps us to see here that to be with Christ, the Lamb, is to be with God, for Christ is the Lord God Almighty who came to us in human form in real time.

## No Need for a Sun or Moon

John next sees an amazing thing about this new city, our future home: "And the city has no need of the sun or of the moon to shine on it, for the glory of God has illuminated it, and its lamp is the Lamb" (21:23, NASB). Here we see the ultimate fulfillment of Isaiah's expectation: "The sun will no more be your light by day, nor will the brightness of the moon shine on you, for the Lord will be your everlasting light, and your God will be your glory" (Isaiah 60:19, NIV).

Yes, we have all of this in picture language. But the eternal truth for us here is that reality can be seen and understood only in the light of God's presence.

A city ablaze with light—one in which there was no darkness, a symbol of fear—would have been an amazing idea to John's first readers. Their cities at night were dark and foreboding. They could enjoy nothing of the thrill we experience when flying over Los Angeles, Chicago, or New York at night—a sight that is a faint reminder of what John saw in the new city.

### All Barriers Are Gone

This new light of God's presence attracts "the nations" and the "kings of the earth" (21:24, ESV). And having said that, John moves on to speak of the inclusiveness of this "new" city: "On no day will its gates ever be shut, for there will be no night there" (21:25, NIV). All former earthly barriers between people have disappeared, and the distinctiveness of everyone is honored.

What a beautiful idea! In God's new world everyone shares in the light of God's presence. No one is barred because of being disadvantaged or the "wrong" color. Each of us will be everything that God intends for us to be.

## The New Relationship—Eternal Life in God's Presence (22:1–5)

John seems to save the best for last as we move into this closing scene with him. Here we get a peek into what it will be like to live in God's presence forever. And once more the symbolism in John's description moves to majestic heights.

### The River of Life

First, John sees "the pure river of water of life, clear as crystal" (22:1, KJV). Here at the very end of our Bible we have a direct reference and connection to the first part, the Garden of Eden scene where a "river flowed out of Eden to water the garden" (Genesis 2:10, ESV). The beginning of God's plan for humankind is in the Genesis garden, and now its culmination is in the "garden city" of Revelation. This river symbolizes the source of eternal life, and since it flows from the throne of God and the Lamb, the supply is endless.

### The Tree of Life

John next sees another symbol of eternal life. On each side of the river there is a tree, or trees, of life, "with its twelve kinds of fruit, yielding its fruit each month. The leaves of the tree were for the healing of the nations" (22:2, ESV). Once again John's vision draws on familiar Old Testament scriptures.

First, we remember the "tree of life" in the Garden of Eden (Genesis 3:22). But the fruit of the tree of life in John's vision was not restricted. There was healing even in the leaves.

Second, we get an even more direct connection between John's description and the words of Ezekiel the prophet: "Fruit trees of all kinds will grow on both banks of the river. Their leaves will not wither, nor will their fruit fail. Every month they will bear fruit because the water from the sanctuary flows to them. Their fruit will serve for food and their leaves for healing" (Ezekiel 47:12, NIV).

In all of this we see God's endless provision of nurture and healing. What great good news this assurance had to be for those first-century Christians who because of their refusal to worship caesar were denied the means of earning a proper living. Here they are assured of God's bountiful supply to meet their needs. To those who suffered from disease and the crippling effects of persecution, there is the promise of healing. And we twenty-first-century Christians share in that same legacy.

### God and Christ Are There

Third, John sees the assurance of eternal life there because of the presence of God and of Christ (22:3). Heaven—perfection—is where God and Christ are. And then John adds, "His servants shall serve him" (22:3, KJV). We're not told here *how* we will serve God, but we are told that we will. It is clear, though, that we will worship Him and share in His reign, whatever that means.

Next John writes that we'll not only serve and worship God, but we "will see His face, and His name will be on [our] foreheads" (22:4, NASB). We will see God and be clearly identified as belonging to Him. Our citizenship in heaven is validated by His name on our foreheads. You will recall that back in the Exodus and Mount Sinai story, Moses was forbidden to look at the face of God (Exodus 33:20). But in God's new heaven and new earth our relationship with Him is so complete that we will "see His face."

In verse 5 the vision returns to the light image as John writes, "And there shall be no night there; and they need no candle, neither light of the sun; for the Lord God giveth them light: and they shall reign for ever and ever" (KJV). There is no darkness (no sin) there, because of the light of God.

This reminds us of Jesus's words: "I am the light of the world: He that followeth me shall not walk in darkness, but shall have the light of life" (John 8:12, KJV), and again, "I am the Light of the world" (John 9:5, NASB). Jesus and God illumine our future home for all time!

## The Epilogue—John's Closing Words (22:6-21)

### *The Angel Validates John's Message*
John now moves to set down his final words in what seems to be a rather unconnected fashion. In verses 6 and 7 we have the angelic validation for the truth of what John has written—that it all came from God Himself. Christ reaffirms His Second Coming, and readers are urged to give careful attention to what John has written.

### *Misplaced Worship*
In verses 8 to 10 John clearly identifies himself as the writer of what he had seen and heard. And then in awe and wonder at

all the angel had shown him, John writes, "And when I heard and saw them, I fell down to worship at the feet of the angel who showed them to me" (22:8, ESV). But the angel rebukes John for his misplaced worship and identifies himself as "a fellow servant with you and your brothers the prophets, and with those who keep the words of this book. Worship God" (22:9, ESV).

Then the angel presses the point home that God alone is to be the object of our worship. John knew all too well this important truth. In the awesomeness of the moment John had bowed down before the angel, and it is possible he has given us this scene to illustrate the danger of misplaced worship. God alone is to be the object of our worship—not family, vocation, charismatic political leaders, pastors, television evangelists, or even Scripture.

### How God Reveals Himself

The next verses (6–10) remind us of how God reveals or shows Himself to us. God chose people—the prophets of the Old Testament and the apostles of the New Testament—to be His messengers. He works through them, using freely their personality traits and writing skills to pass on to us the eternal truths of our faith. And one of the marvels of our study is to see how the words of the Old Testament blend with the New in validating truth. Our Bible is one book. The New Testament writers were intimately acquainted with the writings in what we call the Old Testament. They constantly referred to it and quoted from it. This is precisely why we, as students of God's Word, need to devote study to all of it.

In our Revelation studies John has been the speaker, but his voice is the Voice of God. The book of Revelation is a message given by God to Christ, by Christ to the angel, by the angel to John, and by John to us. We can be certain that nothing was lost in this process—what we have from John is the direct message from God.

### God's Colony in the World

John next makes a very important statement, even though on the surface it may seem a bit difficult to understand: "Let the one who does wrong continue to do wrong; let the vile person continue to be vile; let the one who does right continue to do right; and let the holy person continue to be holy" (22:11, NIV). This does not imply that we should ever believe it is too late for sinners to repent and so just ignore them, even though it is true that some people seem utterly devoted to evil. It is our role as Christians to remain faithful in our witness to them.

John wanted those beleaguered Christians in the Asian churches to be "God's colony" in their world of hardship and persecution. And we in our century, with all of its difficulties and perplexity, are to be "God's colony" in our world. We are to model God's holiness in our speech and actions. We are to support one another in Christian love as we live out our witness in our neighborhoods and towns and cities. It is this that will attract people to Christ and to the Good News of salvation.

### The Second Coming of Jesus

In his next paragraph Jesus is speaking once again to John as he says, "Look, I am coming soon!" (22:12, NIV). Here Jesus is speaking of His Second Coming. The mood of the entire New Testament is that Christ's return will be soon. But how are we to define "soon" in God's terms? When we're children and time seems to drag, "soon" is tomorrow; next year is in the far distant future. But when we reach midlife, next year is soon.

Our human minds find it impossible to see time from God's perspective. But it isn't important for us to do so, and it is certainly supreme arrogance for us to try to put a stopwatch on God's program. What is important, though, is that we live every day in a responsible way as a daughter or son of God. Let's leave the timing up to Him, for in terms of the eons of time, "soon" may be another ten thousand years.

### Christ—the Alpha and Omega

But of this we can be sure: Jesus is, as He says, the "Alpha and Omega, the beginning and the end, the first and the last" (22:13, KJV). Here we have the idea of His completeness, of the fact that He has existed from eternity to eternity, and His authority as judge is unquestioned, for as He says, "I will give to each person according to what they have done" (22:12, NIV). It is He who gives the faithful—those who keep the commandments—"the right to the tree of life" (22:14, NASB), and it is He who judges the murderers and fornicators and liars (22:15).

Jesus then authenticates the accuracy of everything John has seen and heard in his visions (22:16), as He identifies Himself with the prophet's word, "Then a Shoot (the Messiah) will spring from the stock of Jesse [David's father], and a Branch from his roots will bear fruit" (Isaiah 11:1, AMP). As a descendant of David, Jesus is the fulfillment of that prophecy.

### The Great Invitation

Next Jesus continues with the grandest invitation of all time as He draws on the words of the prophet Isaiah, "The Spirit and the bride say, 'Come.' And let the one who hears say, 'Come.' And let the one who is thirsty come; let the one who desires, take the water of life without cost" (22:17, NASB). Here is the great call for every Christian to be a witness by words and actions. And here, too, is the open invitation for all who have not received Christ as their Savior to do so.

### An Important Warning

Immediately following the invitation to participate in the Good News, a final warning is given. It was common practice in ancient times to warn a copying scribe against changing any words in the process. And so in verses 18 and 19 John warns against adding to or taking away from the truth of what has been written. This was a most important warning to the late first-century church, which was plagued with the heresy of Gnosticism. And people have changed little over the years since then. Every century has had its share of adders and subtractors who were bent on willful distortions of one kind or another.

### John's Closing Words

The aged John has now come to the end. The visions are over, and Christ has given His last word. One can almost see him looking out across the western sea from Patmos as the fiery glow of the setting sun shimmers on the water. His has been an awesome experience as two thoughts rage in his mind,

"Amen! Come, Lord Jesus! The grace of the Lord Jesus be with all. Amen" (22:20–21, ESV).

Love and grace—the heart of the message and spirit of Jesus Christ. Our pilgrimage through this astounding part of God's Word has been marked by strange and awesome scenes and images. Sometimes the pictures seemed puzzling and grotesque until we broke their code. But the closing words of "come, Lord" and "grace" clearly express each Christian's deepest longing, the fulfillment of all that we live for.

*Savior, my deepest longing is to know You "in the power of Your resurrection," thoroughly and intimately, in every hour of every day. AMEN.*

# DOMITIAN

Domitian is one of the villains of Revelation for his horrific persecution of the Christians of Asia Minor. Pliny the Younger (c. AD 61–113) described Domitian as a madman. While some of the Roman emperors were deified posthumously, Pliny wrote that Domitian declared himself a living deity. Domitian was the third member of his family to rule the Roman Empire—he succeeded his brother Titus, who had succeeded their father, the emperor Titus Flavius Vespasianus, known as Vespasian, who was responsible for the five-month-long Siege of Jerusalem and the destruction of the temple in AD 70. Together, the three emperors are known as the Flavian Dynasty, which ruled the Roman Empire between AD 69 and 96. Domitian was assassinated in September 96, after which he was succeeded by Marcus Cocceius Nerva.

# EPHESUS

It is generally believed that after John was freed from the "concentration camp" on Patmos, after the death of Emperor Domitian, he returned to Ephesus. Ephesus, now part of the Izmir Province of Turkey, is a very old city, having been founded roughly a thousand years before the time of Christ. It was an important economic center in the province of Asia. The city and its famed Temple of Artemis were destroyed by the Goths in AD 263 but rebuilt by Constantine the Great. Christians know Ephesus best for the letter the apostle Paul wrote to the church there. The ruins of the city are an important archeological site, and today it is a popular tourist destination, in part for its well-preserved ruins that hint at the city's ancient splendor, and in part for sites such as the House of the Virgin Mary, traditionally held to be the final home of Jesus's mother.

# *Notes*

# Notes

# Acknowledgments

Every attempt has been made to credit the sources of copyrighted material used in this book. If any such acknowledgment has been inadvertently omitted or miscredited, receipt of such information would be appreciated.

Scripture quotations marked (AMP) are taken from the *Amplified Bible*. Copyright © 2015 by The Lockman Foundation, La Habra, California. All rights reserved.

Scripture quotations marked (ESV) are taken from *The Holy Bible, English Standard Version*. Copyright © 2001 by Crossway Bibles, a division of Good News Publishers. Used by permission. All rights reserved.

Scripture quotations marked (KJV) are taken from the *King James Version of the Bible*.

Scripture quotations marked (NASB) are taken from the *New American Standard Bible*®, Copyright © 1960, 1971, 1977, 1995, 2020 by The Lockman Foundation. All rights reserved.

Scripture quotations marked (NIV) are taken from *The Holy Bible, New International Version*®, *NIV*®. Copyright © 1973, 1978, 1984, 2011 by Biblica, Inc. Used by permission. All rights reserved worldwide.

# A Note from the Editors

We hope you enjoyed *Living with Purpose Bible Study: Revelation* published by Guideposts. For over 75 years, Guideposts, a nonprofit organization, has been driven by a vision of a world filled with hope. We aspire to be the voice of a trusted friend, a friend who makes you feel more hopeful and connected.

By making a purchase from Guideposts, you join our community in touching millions of lives, inspiring them to believe that all things are possible through faith, hope, and prayer. Your continued support allows us to provide uplifting resources to those in need. Whether through our communities, websites, apps, or publications, we inspire our audiences, bring them together, and comfort, uplift, entertain, and guide them. Visit us at guideposts.org to learn more.

We would love to hear from you. Write us at Guideposts, P.O. Box 5815, Harlan, Iowa 51593 or call us at (800) 932-2145. Did you love *Living with Purpose Bible Study: Revelation?* Leave a review for this product on guideposts.org/shop. Your feedback helps others in our community find relevant products.

*Find inspiration, find faith, find Guideposts.*

## Shop our best sellers and favorites at
# guideposts.org/shop
Or scan the QR code to go directly to our Shop